THE MAN
I WAS DESTINED TO BE

THE MAN

I WAS DESTINED TO BE

Addiction, Incarceration, and the Road Back to God

MICHAEL TANDOI

as told to Bonnie Travaglini

WESTBOW
PRESS®
A DIVISION OF THOMAS NELSON
& ZONDERVAN

WestBow Press books may be ordered through booksellers or by contacting:

WestBow Press
A Division of Thomas Nelson & Zondervan
1663 Liberty Drive
Bloomington, IN 47403
www.westbowpress.com
844-714-3454

Because of the dynamic nature of the Internet, any web addresses or links contained in
this book may have changed since publication and may no longer be valid. The views
expressed in this work are solely those of the author and do not necessarily reflect the
views of the publisher, and the publisher hereby disclaims any responsibility for them.

Any people depicted in stock imagery provided by Thinkstock are models,
and such images are being used for illustrative purposes only.

Certain stock imagery © Thinkstock.

ISBN: 978-1-4908-0216-9 (sc)
ISBN: 978-1-4908-0217-6 (hc)
ISBN: 978-1-4908-0215-2 (e)

Library of Congress Control Number: 2013912773

Print information available on the last page.

WestBow Press rev. date: 08/13/2013

To Dad, I made it!

Contents

Preface

IT'S HARD TO KNOW WHERE to begin. This story began over 32 years ago—for me, a lifetime. It isn't all pretty and I'm not proud of all the decisions I made, but I pray that God will help me find the right words to tell you what happened to me and how I made my way back from drug addiction to a clean and sober lifestyle. My hope is that it might inspire some and possibly save others. If just one person learns from my mistakes and understands the life and death consequences of drug addiction, then this story will be worth all the time and effort it took to tell.

If I had to describe my life in three words they would be 'roller coaster ride." The highs were breathtaking and the lows were crushing. There were twists and turns at every corner and the outcome was devastating. Most of this book was written during my prison incarceration as I reflected on my life's path. This is a true story of eventual success. However, the path was long and arduous. In the end, the real Michael survived and emerged.

My message is simple; love your God, love yourself and know that the sky really *is* your only limit as long as you're clean and sober.

Acknowledgments

THERE ARE SO MANY PEOPLE who deserve to be acknowledged. They stood by me through the hardest of times—when most ran the other way. First and foremost, I have to thank God for giving me a second chance at life and allowing me to overcome the obstacles that always seemed to appear in my life. To Mom, thank you for being the best mom ever. I'm sorry I drove you crazy. You are the strongest woman I know. To Vito and Sal, thank you for being loyal brothers through all of it—now it is time for us to "man up" as Dad would wanted us to do. To Aunt Bonnie, you never stopped believing in me. To my cousin, "D-Rex," thank you for always being there and never changing. Thank you Granny, Jim, and Tammy, you brought me back to life. To Mrs. Conklin, you are my angel from God. To Mike "John," your true and genuine friendship was with me from beginning to end. To Father Weber, Reverend Ellis, and Imam Montiero, your guidance got me through the hardest days of my life. To all the counselors at Mid-State Correctional Facility especially Ms. DiBraccio, thank you for taking a chance on me and helping me beat the odds. Craig, Nicky, Mike, and Joey, my Mid-State brothers, I will never forget you. To Darlene Slack, thank you for your editorial expertise and all you did to help us get this book completed. To Lori, who always said, "Mike you should write a book."

Lastly, a special mention to Thomas "Hollywood" Henderson, whose words not only inspired me but gave me the promise of hope. The "sky is the limit" as long as we're clean and sober.

CHAPTER 1

Payback

LET ME START BY TELLING you that, as I begin writing this book, I am incarcerated and serving a prison term for Assault 2nd, and Reckless Endangerment 1st for a high-speed car chase while I was under the influence of crack cocaine. As a result of the chase, one person was injured but, thankfully, lived through the experience. I have served almost six years of a seven-year sentence in a series of locations in New York State. Currently I am at Mid-State Correctional Facility in Marcy, NY. Truthfully, I don't recognize myself anymore. The change has been astonishing. The person that looks back at me from the mirror is a much better person than the one I used to see. The old Michael no longer exists and I'm relieved that he's gone. I think this might be the first time I've ever recognized the "real" Michael—the one I was meant to be.

Doing time is different for everyone. For me it has been a life-altering experience, the evolution of which has been slow and painful. I know I will never forget "doing time." I don't know how anyone can forget. The change didn't happen right away, and it took a while for me to accept the fact that I actually had an opportunity to make this a valuable and productive time, a time well spent. Incarceration can be a significant learning experience if one is open to its lessons. But it takes a lot to get to that point.

I remember that day so clearly, May 23, 2007. I woke up knowing that today was the day I would receive my sentence and be sent to prison. I was worried sick and I couldn't think straight. My thoughts and feelings collided like trains going head-on at full speed. It was like I was trying to pack for my first vacation but I had no idea what to pack, so I packed everything I owned so I wouldn't forget something. But, when you pack for prison, you don't take anything with you. As soon as you become "State Property," you are stripped of all possessions, even your name. I became a number: 07B-1804.

My brain was working overtime. I can honestly say that there were few things I actually feared, but that day I was terrified. I had no idea how bad the outcome would be and all I knew was Judgment Day had come. Within the next few hours my fate would be decided by a judge who was preparing to sentence me according to the picture that had been painted from the excerpts of my long criminal record. I wanted to say good-bye to everyone but I couldn't accept the reality that I would actually be leaving. So I didn't say good-bye to anyone.

First things first, I had to protect my habit. I knew that "reception" at the county was the absolute worst. The only way I knew how to survive was to figure out how to "smuggle" in what I needed. I was in an all-out panic. All I wanted to do was cry. How did I let my life get to this point? I made some poor choices that led to some really bad outcomes, and now I had to face the consequences of those choices.

We finally got to the courthouse and it was filled with reporters, cops, civilians, judges, my family, and me. As soon as we arrived I could feel freedom seeping out from my body. I felt as though I was being swallowed up. My mind was racing; why am I entering this building? Why can't I just run? I'm out on a $50,000 bail bond. What, Dad, are you saying I'm not worth $50,000? Just let me run. I swear I will pay you back one day. Please, I don't want to go. I won't do drugs anymore; I won't commit any more crimes. I promise! I'll change right now. Please, oh, please!

I can still remember the smell of the courtroom. It smelled like a graveyard to me. The sounds were still and slow. I felt like I was in the center of a deep, deep hole. I could only look up and there was no place for me to go.

Right at that point of my despair our family attorney arrived. If you have ever seen the movie, *My Cousin Vinnie*, my lawyer looked like the first attorney the guys hired, the one who, whenever he had to speak, would stutter. Yes, that was my lawyer. His instructions to me consisted of, "The more you apologize the less time you'll get." My stomach was in knots. My former attorney was the best. He always had a deal worked out before we ever got to court. He would have known how to get me off. He would have been able to tell me what to say, what not to say. But this time was different. I had "gotten off" too many times before. I had every chance given to me. This wasn't my first offense; by this time I had over 100 charges. I had spent half of my life thinking that laws were for everyone except for me. I wonder if even my old lawyer could have worked his magic that day. I will never know, because he wasn't here with me. He, too, was in jail because he bought stolen paintings. It's only now that I can look back to see that this was *the* defining moment of my life. This was the very moment in time that began the evolution from a punk kid to a grown man. It was that *one* crucial change in the equation that would change my life forever. This was the start of payback time.

My current lawyer was not the type of criminal attorney I was used to having. I knew I was in trouble! My family and I entered the courtroom and all eyes were on me. I was the big case of the morning, and reporters ate up my story. The high-speed 120 mph chase made the papers and the local TV. The District Attorney was determined to make an example of me. So the news people were all over the place.

My head was spinning, sweat was pouring off of me. I had to pull myself together for the sake of my family. I couldn't show them my fear. My mother and father were on edge like I had never seen them before. They must have had a sense that things wouldn't go well. As we sat and waited for the judge to appear, I noticed the guy sitting next to me. Rather, I could *feel* him sitting next to me. Then I noticed the woman who sat on the opposite side of my father. I could *feel* her presence, too. They were both there to cover the story and I felt their stares go right through me. They watched my every move, trying to read into my movements and facial expressions.

As my girlfriend and I sat holding hands, I could feel her fear and almost hear her heart pounding. She leaned over to me and said, "Michael, I'll be there for you, I promise." I knew she meant it, but I still wondered how we would continue a relationship while I was incarcerated. We had only started dating three months earlier. We had so much fun together. From day one we both could just be ourselves. Everything came so naturally. I think we both fell in love instantly. I didn't know what to say to her. Of all the people in the world she could have bumped into one day on a sidewalk, it had to be me. I was consumed with sadness.

Then I heard the bailiff say, "The State of New York versus Michael Tandoi." God, help me, please help me. I stood. I thought about running for the door. I thought about dropping to my knees and begging for forgiveness. I *was* sorry, I was so truly sorry. I had been high on crack cocaine. How could I be held responsible for this crime? It wasn't me; it was the monster that lived inside me. The monster called CRACK. All of a sudden I heard the judge say, "Mr. Tandoi is there anything you would like to say before I sentence you today?" "Yes, Your Honor there is." That's when I spoke. I apologized. I expressed how sorry I was. I spoke about forgiveness. I said I was sorry to each of the town police departments that were involved in the chase. I apologized to the injured victim. I even apologized to the judge. I would have apologized to every man and woman in the courtroom that day if I thought it would have helped. I told the judge that I didn't have any control over who I had become. I explained that I had a $1,200-a-day crack cocaine habit. I needed help. I needed rehab, not prison.

All I could do then was stand there and await sentencing. My eyes fixed on the judge, meeting him eye to eye. I felt my heart pounding in my throat. At first the judge talked about two- and one-third to seven years for reckless endangerment, and I jumped for joy inside because I expected much more time. For a minute, I actually believed I had talked my way into a lesser sentence. I could do two- and one-third to seven years, right? That was nothing. I looked back at my mother and father and gave them a look of relief. That's when the judge gave me the absolute maximum sentence the law allowed.

"Mr. Tandoi, you come from a good family, you have a lot of family support and that's why I'm sentencing you to the maximum of seven years. The State has the best programs. You can take advantage of them if you choose, but I recommend you learn everything you can, so that one day you can finally become a man and a productive member of this community. But at this moment in time…*you are a danger to society*."

Danger to society; how could I be a danger to society? *Seven years* flat, with five years of post-release supervision. My stomach sank to my feet. My heart dropped as if I had been pushed off a 20-story building. I fought with every bit of strength I had to hold it together. My parents dissolved into tears. Everyone who was a part of me was in tears. I would have been in tears, too, if I hadn't been so stunned. I felt paralyzed. This was lights out for the first time in my life. I always thought I was above the law, beyond its touch, beating one offense after another. But, I'm all alone on this one. No one can cover for me and no one can bail me out. All the years of ignoring the rules brought me to this point, and now it's time to pay the piper.

I turned to give my family one last hug only to be stopped by a county sheriff who handcuffed me and pulled me away. The snap of the handcuffs shocked me back to reality. As I was led away, I turned around to take one last look at my family, and I shouted out loud, "Mom, Dad I love you. I'll be all right, I promise, it's going to be all right. I love you all. Bye." I remember feeling like a kid being torn from his mother's arms on the first day of kindergarten; all alone and terrified of the unknown. Just thinking back to that day brings chills to my body.

As if life hadn't gotten bad enough, hours after I was processed, my cell got searched. I honestly thought I had done a really good job of getting through jail security during my strip search, as I was carrying my first jail house "smuggle" inside of me. I finally decided it was time to take a couple of Vicodin, smoke a cigarette and think about what just happened when my cell got busted by three commanding officers and a Sergeant asking, "Where are the drugs"? They said, "Listen, Tandoi, we know you just got a ton of time but we also know that you've got a load of drugs on you and it's considered contraband. So, either we can do this the easy way or the hard way. We can promise you won't like the hard way." I can't believe I had to hand over the survival kit that my brother and best friend literally packed for me. But, I was busted once again, and I had to hand it over and suffer the consequences.

Things were so different this time. There was no one to call for bail and no one to come to my rescue. I had signed out my clothes and wallet to my mother as the last bits of the person I was slipped out of sight. As I stood in my cell, I tried to think about how I had gotten here. When did I start the journey down the wrong road?

I thought back to my childhood days, when I was young, innocent and ready to try just about anything. I remember going into the local grocery store to get a fresh blast of helium from the balloon making machine. My friends and I were just being cool. The helium from that canister was actually what started me and my crew of friends down the twisted path leading to nowhere. It was just the beginning of a long list of experimental drug use. Some of us made it out, but we all sacrificed a part of our childhood. How could I have ever known that the first time I sipped a crazy horse malt liquor my life would turn out like it this?

It was just like the 40 days Jesus spent in the desert with the devil. The devil promised Jesus everything. The whole world could have been His, complete with all the kingdoms, palaces and fame. All Jesus had to do was bow down and praise Satan.

That describes the beginning for me. I saw a fun life, filled with fame, money, women, and most importantly, power. Little did I know I was opening the doors to evil and weakness; creating one void after another by chasing one drug only to seek the next even greater high.

Looking back to when I was 15 years old, I can see me and my neighborhood crew smoking pot. We were just kids having fun. You see, I thought these were the harmless years of my life. But, now when I look back, I am able see what was actually stolen from me. Or, I guess I should say what I threw away. I was an excellent basketball player, one of the best in the neighborhood. I thought I was Michael Jordan. I raced my dirt bike and snowmobile and I had a knack with car stereos. But little by little those things became unimportant to me. It all sort of faded away and just left my world. Pot wasn't even my drug of choice, but it was the key that unlocked the world of false dreams. Next thing I knew I was snorting cocaine with the guys on Friday nights. At 17, you would have thought I was right out of the Godfather movie. I wore a leather coat, gold chains and slicked-back hair. I walked around like the world was mine. Add cocaine to the mix and I was out of control. My friends Mike and Johnny, my brother, Sal and I would drive around town in Johnny's Lincoln town car listening to music and snorting cocaine every Friday and Saturday night for what seemed like years. For some reason we thought that was perfectly acceptable because we were Italians. Isn't that what the movie portrayed? Wasn't that our heritage? I can't believe my behavior disgraced so many hard-working Italian immigrants, whose greatest legacy was honor and integrity. Why didn't we see that then?

Today, Johnny is doing great working in construction, but he, too, ended up with a three-year prison sentence. My brother, Sal, is a recovering addict who struggles every day. He's lost many years of his life to drug use.

Mike was killed in a car accident with no fault of his own, but we still lost him and he was such an amazing person. I honestly thought I was on top of the world and my friends came along for the ride. I mean, why not? We had everything, didn't we? From the outside looking in, that's what everyone thought. But if I could have accepted the truth at that point, I would have had to admit that I was miserable. Inside of me, I was dark and lonely. I was constantly chasing the next best thing. When pot wasn't enough, there was alcohol; when that wasn't enough, next came ecstasy, acid, cocaine and girls, girls, and more girls. It was never enough let alone too much. But I had to go a lot further down the road before I would realize that.

However, at this point of my life, I felt sick inside and all I wanted to do was cry, but that would have made things even worse. I couldn't show any weakness now. I had to keep up the persona I had built because the county jail was no playground. The first days were horrible. The worst days of my life, or at least that's what I thought up to that point. I was in City 2C Block. I could hear the sound of inmates throwing up in their cells in fear. They had no idea what would happen to them. Then there were those inmates who had to go through detoxification while in the county jail. I heard them crying and screaming out as they held their aching bodies for dear life. I truly thanked God that I wasn't going through "detox" this time around, but I had other things consuming my mind that made me feel almost as bad. I wasn't dealing with drug withdrawal because I had been clean for a couple of weeks, but I was equally as lost and as broken as they were. I had to face the fact that no matter how talented I may have been, any hopes for the near future were now flushed down the toilet. The worst thing was accepting the fact that I had brought so much shame to myself and disappointment to my family. I had no idea how I would spend seven years alone in a cell. I began missing everyone I ever knew. Sleeping and eating was impossible. Block 2C was not only filthy, but I was the only white guy and I got tested by the inmates as soon as I hit the floor. I did my best to get along with everyone and I did make it out of there in one piece.

Ten days later, at 5:00 a.m., I woke up to the sudden clamor of my cell door shaking. There was an officer standing there with a net bag telling me to get up and pack up my things because I was getting transported to state prison. The reality of my fate was that this was the day I would actually get sent off to state prison to begin serving my sentence for a crack cocaine relapse that will cost me everything I ever worked for. I don't know what to think, all I could feel was my heart racing from the startling sound of the cell shaking and my blood coursing through my body. I was nervous, scared, but most importantly, I was lost. Being confused is one thing, but I was completely lost. I had entered a world I had no business ever entering, and by the time I could reflect on my life, it was way too late. I had no idea what was ahead for me.

I was taken down to a holding tank with 12 to 15 other inmates who would be my "travel companions." We got to know each other by comparing crimes we had committed, judges we had appeared before and the sentences we received. It went something like, "Hi Guys, they call me Tandoi and I got a seven flat for Assault 2nd. My judge was Judge Jones." Look at me. Look how cool I am.

Can you imagine how even at the worst times of our lives we find ways to glamorize really bad situations? As if that glamorization were some kind of feather in our cap and that we still maintained even the smallest amount of dignity. I was in the tank with drug dealers, weapon carriers, rapists, murderers, addicts, and petty thieves. This was the day of reckoning for all of us. No matter where we came from, who we were, how much or how little we ever had, at this moment in time we were all equal. Stripped of all rights and shackled one by one we were escorted to a bus that had the words "State Prison" written on the side. This bus was one of a kind, not like any Greyhound Bus you have ever seen. This bus was built for as much discomfort as possible. It made the journey as unpleasant as it could be.

The first stop was Wendy Maximum Correctional Facility. This was the processing center for the Livingston County Hub for New York State.

Basically, it was a stop-over point. We got haircuts, a bagged sandwich and some face screaming by an over-the-hill commanding officer. If processing got backed up, you got the pleasure of spending the night. Actually, the cells at Wendy weren't so bad compared to the next stop. I have to admit that the pillows at Wendy were the most comfortable I've had in the past six years. I'm sure that was done on purpose and I think there was some kind of strange perversion to it because that would be the last bit of comfort we would feel for a very long time.

The next stop was Elmira State Correctional Facility—Maximum Security. This facility has the distinction of being one of the worst in New York State and it was referred to as "The Hill." This was the real start of "payback" time. I swear on my grandmother's soul, I believed my life was about to end. Complete darkness loomed over this place and to use the term "living condition" was a far cry from anything one might recognize as "living." While we waited our turn for processing, we were placed in human-sized dog kennels. We got called ("we" meaning the entire holding tank of about 50 new inmates) three hours after our arrival. We walked single file to the processing area. Each and every time you enter a new facility, you get re-processed. Each and every change of status requires yet another processing procedure.

Somehow through the grace of God, I was chained up with a guy from my hometown, Rochester, NY. "Stan the Man" broke down the rules of prison life for me, the prison rules that all inmates live by. He would be my saving grace at Elmira. We were escorted across the prison, and led outside to a cut-through path to another part of the building. Elmira is a huge, menacing, medieval-looking place. We got to a gate that unlocked with the loudest locking device I have ever heard. It is a sound that echoed through my body and one sound I often remember because it is one that is not easily forgotten. Each step of the way was one step deeper into despair and doom.

As the door opened, we found ourselves in A-Block reception. It is a cavernous gallery—four tiers high on both sides of me. These tiers had row after row of prison cells. I heard prisoners yelling, screaming in distress, screaming just to scream. I saw "fishing lines" made from torn bed sheets weighted by a bar of soap or something heavy so it could be dropped from the tiers either to pass or to catch some sort of prison contraband. Even today, when I close my eyes, I can see myself standing in the row of 50 inmates in the middle of that gallery. We walked between two yellow lines painted in the center of the aisle. Walking between the lines was the only way you could keep a safe distance from the prisoners living in cells lining the walls.

I could hear the sound of birds flying through the air. I saw mice or rats running around like they were lost and searching for a means of escape. As I took in this shocking scene, out of nowhere I heard, "Tandoi, Tandoi. Hey, man, it's Tandoi"! I had been in reception less than five minutes and I heard my name being yelled in this chamber of horrors. How do these people know me? One by one there must have been six guys greeting me from all over the tiers. "Tandoi, we've been waiting for you; I'll meet you in the yard tonight; I used to go to your club, or I knew you through a friend." I didn't remember any of these guys, but somehow they knew me. I thought I was scared before, but now my heart pounded in terror.

Elmira turns you upside down and inside out with emotions. In all the times I had been in jail, I never imagined there was a place like this. Survival here teaches you to adapt—fast, really fast. If you don't learn to adapt, you can spend day and night tossing and turning, letting it slowly drive you crazy. The only reason I was able to sleep was because of the medication I received to combat my drug addiction.

There was one doctor in the Monroe County jail (my home county) who thought it might be in my "best interest" to give me a prescription for Seroquel. This medication is an atypical antipsychotic medication approved for the treatment of schizophrenia and bipolar disorders. My first interview with this doctor went something like this: (Doctor) "Mr. Tandoi, what seems to be the problem"? (Me), "Well Doc, I'm seeing things, hearing voices and I can't sleep." (Doctor), "I can't imagine why you might be experiencing these things but I believe I can help you." (Me)"Doc, you look familiar." (Doctor) "Yes, I'm sure I do. I know who you are, Mr. Tandoi. You and your friends used to hang out on the side of my house and have your drinking parties at my next door neighbor's house. I used to pick-up all your empty beer cans and trash." (Me) "Oh no, Doc, I'm really sorry about that. I hope you can forgive me." (Doctor) "Oh, yes, Michael, I can forgive you and I'm going to take care of your little problem of imaginary voices, visions and sleep disturbances. I'm going to prescribe a medication for you. Take care, Michael."

Little did I know that 500 mg of Seroquel should have knocked me down for good! That large of a dose, I learned later, could have killed a full-grown horse. You might think I'm a bit paranoid, but I believe that doctor didn't want to forgive me—he wanted to get even with me. But I learned to use the meds to my own advantage. I learned how to exist in these horrendous conditions. I would save the meds until bedtime. If I went to bed at 11 p.m., I could take the meds throughout the night and sleep. My behavior from the meds made me act nothing less than crazy, but it was the only way I could sleep through this horrible place. Besides, "crazy" at Elmira was actually normal.

Elmira was a 21-hour-a-day lock down. I was out of my cell for meals, which only lasted about 15-30 minutes. We also had an hour each day for recreation in either the indoor gym or the outside yard. I actually looked forward to going to meals because I'd never experienced anything like this place before; single-filed lines, cameras everywhere. You could see rocket ball chambers that were poised to shoot hundreds of hard steel balls at inmates if a riot ever broke out. I'm sure if you got hit in the eye with one of these steel balls you would lose the eye.

Standing in line to get your food was like an open market. You could purchase anything you wanted from pornography to cigarettes. This process was called the "in- prison hustle." There were guards everywhere, but we could make this kind of "transaction" as long as we "put some shade on it." That meant we could get away with it if we weren't obvious about it. I found the whole process amazing.

But each day, the realization that my own actions caused me to be put in this situation was an eye opener and left me with a deep sense of sadness and depression. I no longer could enjoy delicious five-course Italian meals. Here, you got one or two scoops of slop, a cup of juice, four pieces of bread and off you went. Each time I went for meals, I had to re-enter the gallery with tiers of cells and the cacophony of clicking, popping, yelling and shaking of cell doors. You could actually feel the vibration of the clamor deep inside your body. It was like the rumble of a jet just before take-off. At the very top of the gallery there was a painting of a Tasmanian devil twisting around like a tornado. I always wondered why they chose to have that painting there. Maybe it was because they wanted a constant reminder that life would be a tailspin for the entire time you were here. This was by far the darkest, coldest, most dismal and lonely place on earth.

We were only allowed to shower three times a week, so at night, special inmates would come around and pour hot water out of a garbage can so you could wash yourself. We each kept a bucket in our cell so that we could get a bucket-full of hot water. I had to soap up and rinse off with that one bucket of water. If you don't do this right, you can make a mess of your cell. So you need to actually stand over your toilet and give yourself a very careful bird bath. I remember feeling so degraded by this ritual. But, again, I was facing seven years. I had to adjust; I had to get down with the program. Checking out of this hotel wasn't an option.

Mice, rats, birds, cockroaches, bed bugs, spiders, you name it, and I am sure it lived at Elmira. The place was filled with the worst of the worst, and now I was considered one of them. Some days I got to go outside and spin the yard, play basketball, work out or just smoke cigarettes. Usually I talked with Stan and we would spend the hour talking about the "rules." What things we could do and what things we couldn't do. Who you hang with and who you don't. He would say, "If you gamble, make sure you have the money and don't get in over your head. You can have fun, but just be safe." The main rules of prison life are:

#1 Don't do drugs

#2 Don't get involved with drugs

#3 Don't get involved with gang drama

#4 Stay away from the chumps

Now, there was one more rule that Stan forgot to tell me about or maybe he just omitted. But I learned that one on my own. You see, you are only allowed to shop the prison commissary once every two weeks. When you first get to Elmira, it takes at least two weeks to get your account set up so you can shop for essentials. This is like a "bank" account that family members or friends can deposit money into for inmates to use. Some inmates don't have anyone sending money so they never shop unless they have a "job" and get a prison paycheck from the State. I was fortunate to have an account. But until this account got established, I ended up having to "borrow" from the "2 for 1 prison store" run by inmates. I was borrowing Newport cigarettes one for two. For every one I borrowed, I owed back two cigarettes. I ended up owing this guy, "House", an entire pack of cigarettes. I intended to pay him back but he got drafted out of Elmira and was sent to another prison. Before he left he told me to pay his cousin. "No problem, "House", I'll pay your cousin as soon as my account is active."

Well, come to find out, his "cousin" was no cousin and I decided I was not going to pay him back. I gave him a line of crap and told him I'd have to see him later. But, I had no intention of paying him back at all.

The very next day I was in the shower room with about 40 other inmates and I saw at least six guys start to approach me, I could see that one guy was carrying a "banger." A banger is basically a weapon; any type of item that could cause harm or even death. Well, the main guy asked me if I was planning on paying "Peaches." I thought to myself, do you really expect me to pay back a guy named Peaches? I didn't ask the question and it was a good thing because I saw Peaches approaching and immediately realized that all these guys are also his "friends" and they are ready to kill me for a pack of Newport cigarettes. Being me I said, "Hey guys, I've been looking for Peaches all day. I have his pack right over there in my pocket." Smiling from ear to ear, I said, "I'll go get it right now." Moving to my clothes, I thanked God for saving my life while consciously realizing that I was being given a chance to live another day.

I could have gotten myself into a real mess that day if I had gone through with my plan. The only person to get stiffed that day would have been me. In prison, people don't help people who are doing others wrong—even if they're named Peaches.

Rule #5: It doesn't matter who you borrow from, you always pay back.

Most importantly, you pay back the chumps; those are the guys that have all the inside juice in prison. *Lesson learned!*

As I said, Elmira is a hub for NYS and it is usually a "stop-over" place. That was lucky for me because I was there only from early June until the beginning of July, 2007. After Elmira, I was transferred to Groveland Correctional Facility near Sonyea, New York. The day I got off the bus at Groveland I was amazed by the beautiful scenery. The place was even more beautiful to me because I had just spent a month at Elmira where the scenery is anything but beautiful.

That day, there were hot air balloons flying overhead and I could see golf carts everywhere—on the other side of the fence. Within my first 24 hours, I met a guy I'll call Jimmy, who filled me in on things. He basically told me how to move in a place with unlimited "movement." Movement is the means by which inmates are allowed to go from one point to the other. You can't just go when you want to, you have to be escorted and there has to be security posted along the way. But at Groveland, there was no "movement" requirement. He also told me that if I was a good worker I might be able to get a job working on the golf course and a chance to be a caddy and drive the carts around.

I actually believed him because I saw inmates doing all kinds of things. There were inmates whose actual jobs were to push wheelchair-bound inmates around. So driving a golf cart didn't seem out of whack to me. I couldn't wait to be able to call home to tell my Mom and Dad about this. As I was telling my parents about this development, there was a guy listening to my conversation. He looked at me like I was crazy and said, "Tandoi, you can't drive a golf cart, whoever told you that was pulling your strings." Okay, so I got played that day!

At Groveland, I was still taking the Seroquel. I would stand in line outside the medical building each evening at 7:15. Half of the jail stood in this line. It reminded me of one big legal drug house. By 8:30 p.m. I was totally looped and in another world. I would lie down on the grass and look up at the sky and hallucinate. The stars would move around like meteors and I would see spaceships and UFOs. I was a mess. I would find myself eating all kinds of crazy things. I would eat popcorn with one hand and peanut butter with the other. I would just stick my hand in the jar and scoop it out. The guys couldn't believe what they saw. I would eat jalapenos right out of the can and think nothing of it. No wonder I was drug tested every three or four days. It looked like I was using, but the medication was prescribed for me. I bet that doctor still laughs when he thinks about me on that medication. I decided to stop taking the Seroquel in September, 2007 a few months after arriving at Groveland.

Groveland was not a good fit for me because it was more like a resort than a prison. It was one big yard, no movement restrictions and open dorms. There was even a stray cat that I adopted as my own. Groveland at one time even had its own bowling alley for inmate use. I wasn't there very long but long enough to make a name for myself as the biggest jerk in the joint. I caused a lot of unnecessary crap within the system. I was caught up in maintaining an image that I desperately needed to get out from under. If only I had known that then.

But, how could I change that wise-guy/tough guy attitude when yet again I found a way to glamorize my prison stay? You see, Groveland was only 30 minutes away from my home. My identity followed me. Also, I was "fresh." When you're "fresh" off the streets and so close to home, family and friends have a better opportunity to visit often and support you. My stay at Groveland (which I referred to as "Groovyland") was like Peter Pan's Neverland where growing up was strictly an option. Every weekend I would get lots of visitors. I would try to have two or three visits each day. It was like a revolving door or more like a circus with one act following the other. I was the acrobat that would swing from visit to visit because that's what I thought I was supposed to do. I worked to keep up my old image.

Being so close to home meant my girlfriend could come up to visit me every weekend. We spent the time holding hands and talking but I continued to wonder how this relationship was ever going to survive. To continue a relationship during an incarceration is almost impossible. It is extremely stressful for both people. I wondered how this arrangement could possibly be fair to her. Time wears out everyone.

At Groveland, there was a Commanding Officer who didn't like me. He even tried to hit on my girlfriend. There were times when I got drug tested several times a week. They really tried to push my buttons, and, in those days, I had lots of buttons. I wasn't using drugs and I wasn't selling them but they thought I was flooding the joint. One day, this C.O. got so mad at me that I was transferred out of Groveland the very next day. All in all, that was the best thing to happen to me — a real blessing because I didn't stand a chance of making a change at Groveland. I could never have become the person I am today. Only now can I see how immature I was then. I was the same guy that left the streets and, if I had stayed, I would go back to the streets unchanged. I know I would have gotten into a lot of trouble had I stayed there.

I may not have been dealing in drugs but I was betting on baseball games. Groveland had the best softball games ever. It was the Field of Dreams with money games every weekend. I would bet the sidelines and the players and on a good night I could come away with 10-15 packets of cigarettes which I could use as barter for other things I wanted. I was still a master at "working a room."

The job I got at Groveland was working in the commissary store, which should have been a great job but the lady civilian who worked there was awful. She would yell at me and the Commanding Officer every day. I think it annoyed her that the C.O. and I got along so well. He would tell me stories about how much he loved the idea of flying and how he dreamt of flying through clouds and over waterways. I would imagine that it was possible to fly through the sky like a bird; my choice would be a hawk. How wonderful, graceful and peaceful it must be. Just like Harry Potter who could fly with just a running start. That's when I realized that I wanted to be a part of the sky—because the "sky's the limit." At this point, however, I had no idea how to get there, but at least now I had identified a goal.

This C.O. knew of my family and one of his favorite restaurants was Fratelli's, which was owned by a friend of the family so we had a type of bond. Then, one day he came by and said that the woman at the Commissary was making a big deal out of me working there and it was time for me to find a new job. I think he actually was sorry to see me go.

There was another C.O. who on the weekends would wake me up by throwing lollipops or rolls of toilet paper at me. He would give me chicken off the grill and we even smoked cigars together. I thought for sure someone was going to kill me for being friends with the C.Os. Groveland wasn't Elmira but it was still a prison.

No, Groveland was not a good place for me because I didn't feel any pain; I wasn't hurting; I didn't feel the loss of family and friends. I would never hit rock bottom there. I made a joke out of the word "prison." I knew I would never be able to become the man I was destined to be if I had done all my time there. God had other plans for me, and Groveland wasn't in that plan. I didn't know it then, but the good times at "Groovyland" were about to end.

I was drafted out of Groveland in September, 2007 and sent to Mid-State where I spent the majority of my time. Mid-State is not the country club Groveland was. Mid-State Correctional Facility is located between the cities of Rome and Utica, New York, about two and a half hours away from my home. This distance made it harder for my family members and friends to visit as often. This was the first time that I actually began to feel the loneliness of incarceration; the distance and the isolation from loved ones. It also was the end of my once cherished visits with my girlfriend. She may have stopped visiting me but she never stopped writing or accepting my phone calls.

Even though Mid-State has a maximum security building, it is still considered to be a medium security prison. There's 87,100 feet of coiled razor-sharp concertina wire surrounding the property just in case any of us needed to be reminded that we were, in fact, in prison. It was a dorm-like setting so we did not live in cells. There was movement here but not as rigid as Elmira and not as open as Groveland.

My first two years in prison were an extension of the life I led on the street—with the exception drug use. I hung out with the cool guys—the ones that were respected for all the wrong reasons. I had my hand in everything from blackjack tables and poker games, to football pools and hustling porn books. I was only interested in doing bad things. If it was bad, I wanted in. In truth, I really didn't know what else I should do. It's too bad that I wasted those years—too bad I didn't wise up sooner. I was into everything but none of it was productive. I didn't blend in with the crowd. My actions caused me to stick out like a sore thumb. I had a 24-hour a day red target on my back. Everyone knew me for all the wrong reasons. I still played the role of a hotshot punk. But, I did learn an important lesson in the early years. The less people knew about what you did for a living or how much money you might have been worth, the better it was.

One of my first jobs at Mid-State was on the lawns and grounds crew. I was a snowplow guy in the winter and a grass mower in the summer. Because of this job, I had permission to be outside. One day, I was outside moving back and forth advertising, "2 for 30 flags." Flags are U. S. postage stamps. We used stamps as a means of barter to "buy" things from each other. It was during a snow storm and I was selling my porn magazines like a jewelry guy selling watches and necklaces from the inside of his coat. I had about six porn books on me and that's when it happened. Tap, tap. I turned around 180 degrees and I was face to face with a sergeant. "Tandoi, get yourself out of here"! "Okay, Sarge. Sorry Sarge." And, that was the end of that hustle. Even today, after all these years, that sergeant still asks me, "How's business, Tandoi"?

I was into everything, and betting on football games was one of my favorite past times. I will never be able to live down the 180-name master sheet I got busted with. They said it was the biggest gambling ticket to ever hit the joint. I guess you could say that I never learned how to do anything "a little bit." It never occurred to me that 180 names were extreme. I didn't set out to get 180 names, it just happened. The other thing was it never occurred to me that gambling while in prison probably wasn't a good idea. But, it was all I knew to do. Looking back, it was pretty ironic.

One Saturday night at the end of September, 2008 (Week 5 NFL), I went to the yard to pass out the unit sheets. Those were the master sheets for the dorms so the guys could follow the games and see how everyone was doing as far as the betting went. I was walking back to my unit (my dorm). I was supposed to meet this guy, "Moose", to pass off his house's master sheet, but I never ran into him so I still had one sheet on me. I turned the corner to my building and there waiting for me is my Commanding Officer and his team of "enforcers." All I remember hearing is, "Tandoi, on the wall"! He asked if I had anything sharp on me and I said no. Then he started to search me. Bingo! They found the master sheet, 60 flags and several packs of cigarettes. I was loaded to the gill. "Tandoi, you're under investigation. Cube confinement pending hearing." That meant I couldn't leave my room except to use the bathroom or go to work. I was in lock-down.

A few days went by and I got called down to Building 21, that's like the Capitol in Washington, DC. The top people of the prison work in this building. I thought to myself, why am I going here, this is not the adjustment committee? That's where I should have gone for the gambling infraction. What is going on? I was called into a Lieutenant's office and I noticed my football ticket is on his desk. He said, "This is pretty impressive. You know, Mr. Tandoi, in 25 years of working in this prison I have never seen a football ticket this big." My head spun with all kinds of thoughts, the worst of which was—I am done for it, now!

Then the Lieutenant said, "But that is not the reason you are here today. I want to talk to you about something else." Something else, what else could he want to talk to me about? That's when he showed me an envelope containing a $50 disbursement slip. A disbursement slip is the prison system's form of a check. The slip was signed by me and made out to some lady in New York City that I actually had never met. The Lieutenant asked me who this woman was and I told him that she was my aunt. Let me back-track for just a minute. I quit smoking three years ago, but back then I smoked cigarettes like they were going out of style. If you have to buy cigarettes from the Commissary Store, that purchase goes against your bi-weekly food purchase allotment. I wasn't having that because my food purchase was very important to me. So, I would gamble excessively to support my cigarette habit. One day a friend of mine introduced me to a guy who was selling 14 packs of Newport for $50. Me being me, I talked him into 15 packs for $50. He gave me this address and said that I was the only one in the prison who had this address. For some reason I expected the guy to tell me the truth. Don't know what I was thinking! I must have had a blackout or something which caused me to momentarily forget that I was in prison, and that all of us were *criminals* who don't know the meaning of the word "truth."

Okay, back to the Lieutenant. He asked me again who the lady was and I said, "She is my aunt, Sir, and that money was a birthday present." That's when it happened. The Lieutenant said, "Well, Mr. Tandoi, not only do you have the biggest gambling ring going on in the state but now you're the biggest drug dealer in the joint because your "aunt" is one busy lady." Then he held up over 40 disbursement slips all made out to this women. Unbelievable!! The whole prison is mailing to this woman! Again he asked me, "So, who is this lady." "Lieutenant, with all due respect, she isn't my aunt. I don't know her, I have never met her." "So, who is she", he asked? "Okay, we can't buy cigarettes at the commissary store without it affecting our food buy. So I met this guy in the yard who turned us on to this woman who sends us 14 packs of Newport for $50. It's a great deal and it doesn't affect our food buy." For some reason, he believed me and bought my story. Then he wished me good luck with the gambling ticket. I knew I told the truth. I don't know what the other guys bought, but my buy was for cigarettes.

The very next day I was called down to the Adjustment Committee for the gambling ticket offense. This office is located in what used to be the morgue. In fact, it's referred to as the "death house." The C.O. was waiting for me; he asked for my ID and told me to take a seat and I would be called in shortly. I was really nervous but ready for anything. I was really lucky that the commanding officer that wrote the offense was my regular C.O. for my housing unit. He gave me a Tier II ticket (offense) instead of a Tier III offense. Since this was my first actual ticket, the most punishment I could get was 30 days in "the box."

The "committee" consisted of three of them and one of me. They asked me all kinds of questions that had no relevance to this ticket—at least that I could see. That line of questioning went nowhere and finally the Lieutenant said, "Can you explain this gambling ticket"? I explained that it was all me and it was just a little fun thing. We bet three stamps a person and no one got hurt, it's just for fun, and I'm the only one responsible. In prison, the inmates that are most respected are those who go down for an offense but take no one else down with them. In this case, there were 179 other inmates. I may have gone down for this infraction, but I was the only one to go down. Inmates all over the joint were running for cover the day I got busted. At that time, nobody knew just how much of a stand--up guy I was. But they all found out. No one else was even questioned. Maybe, just maybe, there was a shred of "honor among thieves" that day.

Then the Lieutenant said, "You know I have to put you in the box for this, right"? I replied that I did understand that but I had a couple of requests. If possible, "I would like to ask if I could go to the Building 10 box. I would also like a porter's job and instead of 30 days, would it be possible for the time to be reduced to 25 days"? Well that made him mad and he said, "Tandoi, do you think you're buying a car? I'm putting you in the box for 30 days and that's that"!

The "box" is a "special housing unit." Special housing unit translates to solitary confinement. You are isolated from the rest of the prison population. It is a prison inside a prison. It's called the box because it's an actual 10 x 6 foot box! There is a toilet, a sink, and a door that never opens unless it is opened from the outside. And it rarely ever opens. If you do get a chance to have the door open you have to back into the door, walking with your hands placed behind your back. You then have to place them through a tray slot so that they can be handcuffed. Then, and only then is the door actually opened by the C.O. The tray slot is also used to slide in your meal tray, and if you get mail, the mail is placed there, too. Other than that, the tray slot stays closed. It was during this time that I first began to realize that something had to change and the change had to start with me.

When I got to the box, I put in for the porter job so that I could get out of my cell as much as possible. My dorm C.O. had already made the call for me. Even so, I was still in my cell for at least 21 hours a day. I thought I would lose my mind. Even as a kid, I was never able to sit still so this was torture for me. I even tried to invent stories and play out imaginary war games to pass the time. To make matters worse, in Building 10 you are not supposed to talk. I spent most of the time reading porno magazines. Once I even got caught by the Reverend. It was not a good experience and I can't believe what a jerk I was that day.

I was truly a mess and I seriously wasn't accomplishing anything. I continued to do what I always had done. But now, I was finally beginning to question whether I could live like this for the rest of my life. It was sad, but so true --I was wasting my life away. I was living in the Super Bowl for idiots and I was the captain of the team.

Once I finished my time in the box, I went back to my job on the lawns and grounds crew and tried to stay out of trouble. I was doing my job and getting through the days and the time slowly passed. It was now June 3, 2009 and I called home to talk to my mother. It was the usual, "Hi Mom. How are you, what's going on"? Instead of, "Oh, we're all fine…" I got a hesitation and I just knew something was wrong. I could tell that she wasn't telling me something. So I stopped her in mid-sentence and said, "What's really going on over there"? I never could have foreseen the bomb that she dropped next. "Michael," she said, "your father has had a heart attack and is in the hospital." At that moment, my body froze, I couldn't think at all, and nothing seemed to make sense. "Is he okay?" Up to this point in his life, my father had had five heart attacks. His first was at 35 years of age and now he was 56 years old. I couldn't understand why my Mom hadn't contacted the prison to say my Dad was in the hospital. In prison, if your family member is in the hospital for a serious situation they can set up a visit, but it cannot happen in a matter of minutes. Everything takes time in prison. I started to panic. I never felt so helpless and out of control of events as I did at that moment. A million questions raced through my mind. What happened, and who got him so upset that his heart rate went up? I was so angry. I was angry at my Mom for not telling me, for not calling the prison but I was most angry with myself for not being home when my Dad needed me. I hung up on my mother and I called my stepmom, Janet, to find out the other side of the story, and she told me everything.

My mother had downplayed the seriousness of the heart attack, but I can't blame her for that. I don't think she knew what to say knowing how close I was to my father. I think she feared that knowing about the heart attack would somehow endanger my safety in prison. Janet explained that Dad was scheduled for surgery on Monday, June 8. The doctors needed to stabilize him before they could even think about surgery. It was a very serious heart attack and the chances of survival were not good.

I was sick. How could this be happening? Come on, Dad, I know you're strong and I know you're going to survive this. Remember, this time away was only supposed to be a minor setback for a major comeback. You told me to accept the seven years and you promised me that everything would be okay. You said you would be there for me. Wait a minute; I suddenly realized that this wasn't about me it was about my father.

My Dad was in the hospital fighting for his life. Why didn't he learn from the other attacks? Doctors told him he had to stop smoking, yet he continued to smoke two to three packs of cigarettes a day. The doctor said less stress, and he had me as a son. "I am so sorry, Dad, I never meant for our lives to get out of control like this. I never realized how hard this was on you. I swear, Dad, I won't let you down ever again. Just don't die, you have to make it." I never prayed so hard. "God, please don't let him die. I need him now more than ever, and it's not fair that he has to suffer like this. Please send him healing and strength. Please."

I didn't sleep that night and at 8 a.m. the next morning, I ran down to the prison chapel to see Father Weber, the Catholic priest. He wasn't there, it was his day off, but Reverend Ellis was there and I needed so badly to see someone. I barged into his office, told the Reverend my name and said I needed help. I explained about the heart attack and the risky surgery. I can't wait; I need to see him because he might not make it through the surgery. I have to go today!

Reverend Ellis said, "Okay, Mr. Tandoi. Take a breath and relax. I know you are on edge right now but nothing happens that quickly in a prison. It takes time to set up a visit and we would need his doctor to say that he really is in a death bed situation. Then we need to get you cleared for transport. It usually takes 24 to sometimes 72 hours."

"Okay, Rev, look, please go see all the people you need to see, pull all the juice you can. Meanwhile, I'm going to go talk to the people I need to talk to and together we are going to get me to that hospital today. I have to trust you. Please help me. "

Today, I know that I had nothing to do with the 3 p.m. instruction, "Tandoi, get dressed, you're going on a hospital visit. Go to the charts and get processed." God had all the juice on this one. I truly believe my father said to God, "Ok, God, I'm ready for you but before I go can you please allow me to see Michael one last time." Just like that, God answered his prayer. It must have happened like that because no one ever gets cleared as fast as I did that day. I was out of the front gate by 3:30 p.m. on June 4, 2009. I might have been shackled from hand to waist, waist to legs but I was being transported to the hospital to see my Dad. As long as I live, I will always be grateful to the angels God sent disguised as two NYS prison C.O.s who drove me to see my Dad.

The ride was long because I didn't know what to expect. Mid-State is two and half hours from Rochester. I couldn't grasp the fact that I was in the process of being transported to see my father who was on the verge of death. The feelings I experienced during the ride were unbearable. I never felt so lost and alone. I cried for most of the trip. I had never imagined that my father wouldn't be there when I got home. I just couldn't accept the inevitability that he was about to die. "Dear God, please, just let me get there in time, please."

We arrived at the hospital and my family was there ready to greet me like I was a rock star instead of a prisoner. My mother, two brothers, grandmother, cousins and two close friends were all at the front entrance. For a second I felt sorry for the C.O.s because they had no idea what was in store. You see, my family puts the "dys" in dysfunctional. Janet, my stepmom, and my Aunt Mary were with my Dad. My Aunt Mary, my Dad's younger sister, had been a registered nurse for years and had worked in this hospital for a long time so she knew her way around.

As if walking in to see my Dad who was near death wasn't surreal enough, I was walking into the hospital escorted by two uniformed

Commanding Officers. I was dressed in greens and in shackles. My mind was racing; all I wanted to do was get into the room to see my Dad. As I walked down the hospital hallway, I felt like a huge green monster. People I passed seemed to clear the way for me because they were stunned by the sight. My Aunt ushered me into my Dad's room. There the C.O.s unlocked the hand shackles and let me hug my father. The very first thing he said to me was, "Michael, I knew you'd get here. What took you so long"? I answered, "Well, Dad, the Captain told these wonderful C.O.s that I was not allowed to drive because he heard that I drove way too fast." Then my Dad laughed. If you knew my Dad you would think he had just gotten off the boat after a relaxing day at Sodus Bay. Honestly, he looked good and he had good color in his face. Well, at least I thought he looked good because I was expecting much worse. The whole way to Rochester I worried that he'd be dead by time I got there. I gave him a hug and a kiss and I was allowed to spend two full hours with him. He asked me all kinds of questions and he gave me all kinds of instructions if anything went down and if he didn't make it. My father passed his legacy on to me along with his blessing. All the time, I kept saying, "Dad, you're going to be okay, you're going to make it." He made me promise that I would finish my time, learn everything I needed to learn and become the man I was destined to be. That's when I knew he had no intention of going through with the surgery. He must have known that he wouldn't make it. So I told him that he had permission to go on a vacation, forget about the problems. I promised him that I would make it.

The ride back to Mid-State was even harder than the ride to Rochester. I spent the time reliving my father's life. I thought back to every memory I had. My father would call me at least 80 times a day, without exaggeration. I would answer by saying, "Dad, I just talked to you two minutes ago, or I just told you what I had for dinner or you asked me 10 minutes ago where I was." He would drive me crazy and I couldn't help but wonder if I would ever get another chance to get one more call. Could our visit really have been the last time I would talk to my Dad? What did he really mean when he said, "You need to become a man, Michael"? It sounded pretty easy, but it has turned out to be the hardest challenge of my life. As we drove, I was surprised to find myself starting to prepare for the worst possible thing. My Dad might actually die and he might not be here in the morning. We really did have it all once upon a time not so long ago. The only thing that ever came between us was my drug addiction. I am so sorry I let that steal away the time I had with my Dad. I promised him that I would make it, but the truth was I had no idea how I would make it. But I knew there would be nothing that would get in my way of keeping my promise to him.

If there was one thing we all knew, it was that Dad only wanted the very best for all of his sons. Although he loved each of us for who we were, I was his clone. I was his right and left hand in the family business. Where Dad went, I went. I never wanted to be without my father. He was my idol, my role model, and he was everything to me. Through all of the difficulties and problems I had created for him, my addiction to crack cocaine was the one thing that truly broke his heart. He would say to me, "Michael, you're killing me, you are just killing me." He would hit his chest with his fist and no matter how much my Dad meant to me during my addiction, I could not stop. I wanted to so desperately, but I had lost complete control of myself. That crack monster stole my power to be the son my Dad raised and loved.

It wasn't like I woke up one morning and decided to become a crack addict. One bad choice lead to another and before I knew it, BAM, I was caught up in my own type of death. I was alive but I was dead inside and under a spell sent from the devil. Her name was Crack Cocaine and I let her take me down.

Before I left my Dad, I told him that I loved him. He said, "I love you, Michael." Then he thanked the C.O.s and tried to slip them a $20 bill so they would buy me dinner. My Dad was on his death bed and all he was worried about was me eating dinner. That's the perfect example of what kind of person my father was. He had a million dollar smile and he was full of class and charm. His heart was so big and he would do anything for anyone. And, yes, I am guilty of taking advantage of his kindness more than anyone else.

It was early morning on Friday, June 5, 2009. I was cutting grass, and suddenly I felt it. I was staring up at the sky because the sun was extra bright that morning. The weather was just too nice. I could hear birds chirping. I was on the tractor, and I felt as though "something" had just entered my body. It was a feeling of complete peace and I had the sense that things would be okay. Within 10 minutes of that feeling, I was called down to the Chapel office. This time when I got there, I was met by the Muslim Leader, Imam Montiero. He sat me down and told me that my Dad had passed away. That was it. "Your father has passed."

I was in shock. My mind couldn't grasp the reality—the finality of all of this. It was just so painful. My Dad was gone! I desperately needed someone to hug me, to comfort me but there wasn't anyone. My first emotion was anger. How could God let this happen? Why did He let this happen? He could have made this turn out differently. I was so angry!

I had one "free" phone call courtesy of the state prison system so I called my Mom. I don't remember saying too much to her, I do remember crying a lot. I had a choice of going to see my father while he was alive or I could have attended the funeral. I took the first choice and I am so glad I did. But, this experience was more than I could bear. I know it isn't easy for anyone to lose a family member, a loved one, someone close. But added to the overwhelming sadness I felt, I was overcome with guilt that I wasn't home when it happened, and that made it even harder on me. My being in prison took away two years longer I could have spent with him. That is something I will have to live with for as long as I live.

Five months before my Dad died, I got up one snowy January morning at 5:30 a.m. to get ready for work. I was working the early morning snow crew, plowing snow with the tractor. I went to light up my morning cigarette and my first drag of the morning almost killed me. It felt like my circulation was completely cut off to my heart. I passed out and fell on the bathroom floor. When I finally came to, I was dizzy and very light headed. I couldn't believe what had just happened. It scared me out of my mind and that's when I told myself that there was no way I was going to die in prison! I took my fresh pack of Newport and went back to my room and threw the pack as hard as I could at my boy "Guess." I threw them so hard, I woke him up. He said, "Tandoi, what's wrong with you?" I asked him if he wanted the brand new pack and he said, "Yeah, just leave me alone." I answered saying, "Good, 'cause I'm all done." And just like that I quit smoking two packs of cigarettes a day. That was my very first accomplishment in prison.

John "the plumber," one of my dorm mates would try to set me up to fail by leaving tobacco all over my room. It drove him crazy that I was able to quit smoking. Even when times got tough, especially when my Dad died, I never picked it up again. I never turned to drugs. I dealt with each situation and faced every obstacle no matter how tough it was. I knew it would only be that much harder if I used. Author of _Out of Control: Confessions of an NFL Casualty_, and former football linebacker, Thomas "Hollywood" Henderson wrote, "Life is hard all on its own, now you add drugs and alcohol and life becomes impossible." At times, especially on holidays, I can hear my Dad's voice saying things like, "Come on, kid, smoke just one cigarette." I smile and think to myself, "Sorry, Poppy—that's not going to happen."

Today, I believe that my father's spirit lives inside of me and I have come to accept his loss. But when he died, I was mad, I was so mad at God. I stopped going to Church and even stopped talking to people. I continued to live the only way I knew how. I got in trouble within a month. By July, 2009 I landed back in the box. But this time it was for extortion.

We have all heard the saying, "Insanity is doing the same thing over and over again expecting different results." My question is, how many times does a person have to hit the same wall before he realizes that a certain behavior doesn't work? I have asked myself this very question at least a million times. For the life of me, I could not understand why I continued to get into trouble over the same exact type of behavior. But I did.

Things had just started to calm down after my father's death the month earlier. I was keeping out of the limelight doing my time the best way I knew. I wasn't playing cards or booking sporting events to fill in my time, so I guess I got bored! I had the ingenious idea of opening up my own 2 for 1 Prison Store. I decided to run a coffee shop and cigarette business. Didn't the judge tell me to learn everything I could learn? Wasn't this something to learn?

Where there is a prison, there is a 2- for -1 Prison Store, which is basically a store within a small area of the prison that is run by an inmate. In the house where I lived, I had seniority and I basically called the shots. I went to a couple of guys, told them my plan and everyone was cool with it. I started to stock up on my supplies from the Prison Commissary Store and opened shop. The only time you have to stock up is for your initial buy. After that, your customers supply the stock. Business was booming, sales were up, people were happy. Then "Joe" moved into our house. "Joe," as it turns out, became my best customer. After a month, I only sold to "Joe" because he bought so much, I didn't need any other customers. I wanted the other guys in my house to get in on this, so they took over the 2- for -1 on the items that I no longer handled. Each of us sold something different, and we never crossed the lines. Those are the rules and everyone in prison lives by the rules. We had a full grocery line with potato chips, pepperoni, cake mixes, candy, pies, etc. You name it, and you could buy it from one of us as long as you were willing to pay the 2 for 1 charge.

One day, "Joe" came to me and said that his money hadn't come in yet, so I'd have to wait for the payback. I was okay with that so I waited, and waited. "Joe" still needed his coffee, creamer, sugar and smokes. The next two weeks went by and it's now payback day. Something just didn't feel right. It seemed as though "Joe" was looking for a way out.

By 9 a.m. the next morning, I heard through the prison grapevine that "Joe" had asked permission to have someone help him carry his commissary bags back to his dorm and the C.O. denied the request because "word" had come down that someone was extorting "Joe." He had supposedly signed a waiver that everything was okay but they still moved him out of the house that day. I decided to wash my hands of this guy, cut my losses and learn a lesson. However, the guys still wanted to pursue the issue with "Joe" because he owed all of them, too.

I kept telling my guys it wasn't a good idea, that something would go wrong. They thought I was going soft or just being paranoid. Well, let's just say that there were a couple of guys waiting for "Joe" at the commissary store and they made sure that he shopped for all the items he owed us. His $55 bi-weekly food allotment was spent for the next two weeks. Remember Rule #5: No matter who you owe, you always pay back.

While this "transaction" was going on, I was in my housing unit. Later that day, I was sitting inside our E.A.O organization (European American Organization) getting things ready for our meeting that was scheduled for 6 p.m. I was president so I was there by 5:30 p.m. The guys started coming down and all I heard was, "Tandoi, they got your stuff, they raided your whole room. They tossed everything you own, they even took your food." I couldn't just take off. I had to wait for "movement." Well, "movement" wasn't for another hour and a half. My brain was frozen, I couldn't think. All I could do was to wait for time to pass. My thoughts were out of control. I felt like I just got high. Finally it was 7:30 p.m. and we could finally go back to the dorm.

When I got back to my dorm you could feel the tension, people couldn't get to me fast enough. "Tandoi, they turned your room upside down." At that time, I was living in a four-man room. All four of us were involved in this. So, our whole room got tossed. By time we walked to our room, we could see that the place looked like a hurricane had torn through. What a mess, worse than a house raid. We looked at each other, shook hands and wished each other well because we knew we were in for it. Then instead of cleaning up the room we just sat on our beds and waited for the guards responsible for the raid to come back for us. Sure enough, within 10 minutes, 10 of them took charge like this was some kind of big event at Mid-State. It turned out all four of us would go down for this. They searched us, cuffed us and locked us up. Here I go again!

This time the ticket would be a Tier III offense. Now I am out of my mind. Tier III is the worst thing that could happen to you during your incarceration. It gives the prison permission to sentence you to more torment than you can ever believe. You lose your good time which is your conditional release date. In other words, not only could you get 190 days (or more) of box time but you could also get time added on to your sentence. My conditional release date was February 23, 2013. But with this Tier III offense, I could actually stay in prison until February 23, *2014*. You get extended time, you have to repeat programs and wipe away everything you accomplished up to this point and start over again. Two steps forward, 10 steps backwards. That's how it happens—fast!

After they cuffed me I was immediately taken to the box in 10-Building. During the processing procedure, I was getting stripped searched, and one of the C.O.s that I had previously worked for looked at me and said, "You see Tandoi, I may have had one inch of respect for you before, but now I look at you and see how pathetic you really are. Pick up your crap and get dressed." I felt like the biggest pile of scum ever. The C.O. was mad because, at that point, he thought I was taking advantage of "Joe" because he was an older man. I couldn't utter one word in my defense. I just swallowed my pride and went on my way. I didn't like feeling this way anymore. Even though I wasn't guilty, I felt lower than ever before in my life. He finished by saying, "You inmates are all the same. Hope you don't need anything because you're not getting anything from anyone." I don't know why, maybe it was still the pain of my father's death but, I actually cared what he thought of me.

I was in Building 10 for the first three days and then I got transferred to S-Block. I was shackled to a chain of four other inmates. I got shackled with a guy named "Bam-Bam." He was a short heavy set guy with no hair and missing teeth. He had gotten into a fight with someone, but he didn't fight back and ended up in the box for 30 days. The SHU-200 C.O. dispatched the tower guy to open the gated entrance. Then, all five of us guys were placed in a holding tank so we could get processed—again. This time I remember clearly that the C.O. asked me if I had any thoughts of suicide or any mental health disorders. "No Sir, I'm okay for now." Then we were assigned our cell locations. As luck would have it, I got Bam-Bam as a cell mate. If that isn't bad enough, I get assigned the top bunk. "Bam-Bam" and I got to know each other and it turned out that he was an all right kind of guy. We talked about our past and our future, which at that moment wasn't looking too promising.

The SHU box is dark and either really cold or extremely hot. For me it was hot because I went in on July 1, 2009. I spent part of my time dreaming about the last July 4th I'd spent with my family and friends. I actually turned on the sink faucet to hear the water running. I closed my eyes so I could imagine being on the boat watching the fireworks show at Charlotte Beach. Ask me if it worked, and I'll tell you a lie and say, "Oh, it was just like I was there." I realized how alone I felt with my father gone. The pain from missing him was tremendous.

At the back of our cell, there was a door that opened to a porch. This particular cell was on the second floor so our porch was up in the air and there were cameras everywhere. The way the system worked was three hours a day the showers got turned on and the porch door got opened. This was the way inmates got their one hour of "recreation". One inmate would shower and the other was out on the porch. Everyone would scream and yell back and forth from the porches. Believe it or not, I knew at least 10 other inmates who were in the box during this same time so I was one of the guys screaming and yelling as we talked.

The porch overlooked a big grassy area and beyond the grass there was the road that led to freedom. I could actually see cars and trucks driving by. Once I saw a car of hot chicks that were singing at the top of their lungs probably for the benefit of all of us inmates, but they looked like they were having a great time. Seeing them pass by reminded me once again of the freedom I had lost. I was locked up in a large dog kennel with freedom in my sight but no ability to reach it. I couldn't believe how messed up my life was at that moment. What was going to happen to me?

I was tripping out because of the Tier III ticket and what it could mean for me while my crazy roommate is crying because he got 30 days! I thought I would surely lose my mind. But instead of beating up on "Bam-Bam" and getting another offense, I decided to put him on my defense team. We spent hours upon hours talking about my charges and how I needed to go about proving my innocence on the extortion charge. I must have read the charges on the ticket a hundred times, and each time I came up with another theory and approach. But, each time I read the ticket one thing never changed. It was all based on lies. "Joe" fabricated just about everything. What I didn't know until I read the ticket was that "Joe" was in over his head around the entire compound not just with me or the guys in my house. He did owe me, but what he said was just crazy and totally untrue. I treated him great, extended him credit and never threatened him. No one ever put their hands on him, which "Joe" said we did. He loved his coffee, creamer, sugar and cigarettes and when the price of cigarettes jumped from $.76 to $2.12 a pack and to $3.18 for a pouch of tobacco, I knew there would be a problem. I was never so right.

I think I was especially stressed because *this* time I actually realized how much I had to lose, exactly how much was at stake. This was the very first time I had ever looked at anything in that way. My Dad was gone and there was no one else to turn to. So, I turned to God.

Although turning to God wasn't the usual way I operated, it also wasn't new to me. When I took my first hit of crack cocaine, I found myself existing in a foreign place. The light turned to dark and no matter how hard I tried to get back, I just couldn't. I was trapped in a world that bred lost dreams and washed away promises. I remembered the times that I actually cried out in terror asking God to please protect me. I would run to every church in town. There must have been a least a hundred times my girlfriend called looking for me. The first thing she would ask was, in which church parking lot was I hiding? As high as I might have been, I knew enough to go to church because it was only there that I felt safe.

So, again, I started talking to God. Part of it was so I wouldn't lose my mind, but the other part was I knew I needed help with this one. I had so much to lose. Looking back, I realize that this was another major turning point in my journey.

Whenever I started something new, I never concerned myself with the possibility of failure. I never feared failure. In fact, it never crossed my mind for a second. But now, with my Dad gone, going home was the only thing I could think about. I had to finish my time and go home. Having more time added just wasn't in the picture. I needed all the help I could get and the only one that could possibly help me at this point was God Himself! So I talked to him, I never stopped talking to him. I made all kinds of promises—promises I intended to keep. "Please, God, don't let me go down for this one, please. If you will help me, I will change my ways." So I made a covenant with Him; "Get me through this and I will change my life!"

That's when it happened! I received a letter from a lady, Mrs. Conklin. She was our next door neighbor when I was young. She had never written to me before and this was the first time in 15 years that I had even thought of her. She was well into her 70s by this time, but as a kid, I would always make sure that her sidewalk was shoveled in the winter. No one told me to do that, I just did it. She wrote the most heartfelt, tear-jerking letter I have ever read. That letter turned out to save my life during the hearing. It is without a doubt that I believe a Higher Being had her write that letter. How else could it have arrived at this exact moment of my life?

The day after I received the letter I was called down to my hearing. The knock on the cell door came and the C.O. said, "Tandoi, you have two minutes to get ready. The Captain is here for your hearing." I jumped off the bunk and got dressed as fast as I could. I grabbed all the paper work I needed for my defense and the letter I received from Mrs. Conklin, the Angel of God. As I got dressed, I prayed one last time, "Please, God, help me with this. Stay with me, let me say the right things."

C.O. was back at my door and said, "Turn around, back up, put your hands through the tray slot." He cuffed me and said, "Now back up toward the wall and don't move." I was instructed to lift one leg and then the other. Both legs were shackled and connected to the waist chain and I hopped down to a holding tank that was used for ticket hearings. When you get a Tier III offense your hearing officer is usually a Captain or Superintendent. This was high power for large sentences. I was really nervous, but I sat as relaxed as I could be under the circumstances.

Then the Captain walked in and told me to state my name, ID number and the date. He then read my ticket and asked me what I had to say. As I started to make excuses, he stopped me. "Mr. Tandoi, I want you to know that you can save the line of crap for another day. I know more about you than you know about yourself." I thought, oh no, I'm going down! I spoke to God one more time and said, "Okay, God, please give me the right words for this because I can't do it myself. My way will bury me."

So I began to tell the Captain how the whole ticket was a lie. I explained how one lie led into the next one and how it was not possible for me to have been where "Joe" said I was. I was in my housing unit all day and it was impossible for me to have been in front of Building 27 at 12:45 p.m. Then I asked him to place a call to my first witness who was my C.O. Now, this particular C.O. is known for his strict adherence to the rules. He never bends the rules, not for anyone at anytime. Lucky for me, he was on duty the day in question. The Captain placed the call to the C.O. and I started my defense.

First question: "At 12:45 was I in the housing unit or was I signed out to a program. Would you please check your time-accredibility sheet?" The C.O. responded, "Mr. Tandoi was on the Unit, Captain." Second question: "Did Mr. "Joe" Jones ask you for permission to have someone help him carry his bags from the store"? He answered, "Yes, he did, Captain." "Did you deny that request?" He replied, "Yes, Sir, I did." "After that, did you send Mr. Jones to the Mess Hall to see the Sergeant so he could be questioned about a "snitch note?" "Yes, Sir, I did." "At that same time, did "Joe" Jones deny everything in the note and sign a Protective Custody waiver?" He said, "Yes, he did." Next question: "When Mr. Jones returned to the unit, was it in your best judgment to move him to another housing unit that day?" He responded, "Yes it was." I thanked the C.O. and told the Captain I had no other questions.

The Captain seemed pretty impressed and he looked me over and then asked if I had anything else I wanted to say. I replied, "As a matter of fact, Sir, I do. I would like to read a letter I received yesterday from a woman who was my neighbor when I was a kid. I would like to read it to you because I think it actually came from God."

> *Dear Michael,*
>
> *God bless you always. I know we haven't spoken in a very long time. I just found out that you are in prison. I am so sorry to hear that and I wanted to tell you what a special person I think you are. When you were a young boy you would come over to my house and help me with all kinds of things that needed to be done. You would shovel the driveway in winter and cut the grass in summer. You have so much potential and you have been a blessing to me and to others. I remember how you would come over to ask if there was anything you could do to help me. Whenever I would try to pay you, you would tell me, "Don't worry about it." I hope you can still remember the times I surprised you with your*

favorite brownies. It is time to wake up, Michael. At the end of your sentence, Jesus is waiting for you with His arms wide open. Don't be afraid to find your way through Christ. I know you can do it. You have special talents and abilities to conquer every trial. I will pray each night for you. May God bless you always.

Sincerely, Mrs. Conklin

Once I finished reading the letter, the Captain asked me to remain calm and turn around while he made a phone call. I turned around, but I could still hear everything he said. He called the Sergeant who had arrested us and he reprimanded him like I had never heard before and, in prison, reprimand is an everyday occurrence. When he was done he said, "I can't convict Mr. Tandoi of these charges. I've got to let him go. Case closed"!

I beat that charge, but from that day forward, God made sure that I held up my end of the bargain. That was when my life began its change in earnest. Slowly but surely I started re-evaluating my past life with the hope of discovering a life filled with His love and compassion. I remembered a passage from the Bible that always stuck in my head. It gives us an instruction—if you want to enter the Kingdom of Heaven, you must become a child of God. So, I decided my journey would start there. How would I be able to find that lost child of God?

CHAPTER 2

Looking Back

IT WAS AT THIS POINT, I really began to evaluate my life. I started reviewing the events that had led me into the bizarre and savage worlds of addiction, and ultimately, prison. I think most of us would rather not pay attention to the things we need to do in order to change our lives. Change is hard and facing demons is even harder. But this was a challenge I was ready and determined to face. I started looking back in time, trying to remember some childhood days when I was happy. Not all of my memories were good, but I decided to put the bad ones aside for the time being and just concentrate on the good ones. I felt that was the best place to begin.

I remember waking up every morning begging my father to take me to work with him. In truth, all I ever wanted to do was spend time with my Dad. It was his dream that one day I would take over the business and I think I always knew that.

On my sixth birthday, I was outside in the front yard with my father and Uncle Tweedy. He really wasn't my uncle, but my father's absolute best friend, Jimmy. He was the brother my father didn't have (he had two sisters). I don't know where that name came from but he was always "Uncle Tweedy" and the name always seemed fitting. My Dad kept telling me. "Soon, kid, soon your birthday present will be here." I couldn't believe my eyes when I saw a jumbo flat bed trailer carrying a brand new Hertz 580 Backhoe stop right in front of our house. Now, the backhoe wasn't really mine, but it most definitely was mine for that day. I spent the entire day taking turns going from my father's lap and then to my uncle's lap while they drove the backhoe. I was King of the Road for sure. I could not have been any happier than I was that day.

Birthdays were big around our house. And, looking back, I can remember a big Cookie Monster cake and Big Bird actually showing up for my birthday. I was an adult before I found out that Big Bird was actually my Uncle Rob dressed in the costume that my Aunt Joanne sewed. I had some great childhood memories.

I loved playing sports and I was pretty good at it, too. I had dirt bikes and snowmobiles. I built tree forts and hung out in the woods. I was so happy to be alive back then. My life was great in so many ways. I loved the child I once was but where did that Michael go? Why had that happy-go-lucky little boy disappeared? When did I make the fateful turn down the wrong road? When, where and how did I learn to disrespect myself and everyone else? Where did that behavior come from? So, as I began to search out how to become a child of God, I had to relive some of the other memories I had, the not so happy ones.

I took a hard look back to see if there were any clues. I truly believed that I had lived a charmed childhood. Not until I began to look deeply into my childhood, did I realize that maybe-- just maybe it wasn't so charmed after all.

My quest for clues led to the discovery that I have a borderline personality disorder. In fact, I was surprised to find that I was almost a classic case. This disorder affects how you relate to others, how you feel about yourself and also how you behave. Self-image and sense of self often change rapidly. An unstable self-image can lead to frequent changes in jobs, friendships, goals, and values. As I grew older, I was never satisfied by the way I looked. I realize that every teenager goes through similar experiences, but I was *never* satisfied. I always felt as though I didn't measure up.

Also, I was never able to do anything half way. It was always huge or nothing. I could change directions on a dime and I was always on to the next big adventure. In general, this disorder made it hard to control my emotions, and it was suggested that some of the problem might be a result of harmful childhood experiences. If that sentence had been written in giant red letters, it couldn't have jumped out at me any more than it did.

As I mentioned before, my family is the best dysfunctional family of all time. Every family has its "stuff," and mine wasn't any different except for the fact that, actually, we *were* different. However, I thought we were as normal as they came. Every family had its share of "dirt", but mine did a really lousy job of hiding it.

My brothers and I were literally named after the Corleone Family—Vito, Michael and Sal. Yes, that's right, the Godfather movie!! What made it worse was we actually lived like we were part of the movie minus the killings and corruption. I was the middle child between two brothers. I absolutely did suffer from middle child syndrome. I passionately craved attention. From as long as I could remember, I needed to be recognized for everything I ever did. I was the most aggressive of the three of us and I was extremely attached to my father from the very beginning. My most favorite thing was to cause trouble. And I caused a lot of trouble.

It wasn't until the age of 26 that I found out that I suffered from Attention Deficit Disorder (ADD) and was bipolar! Who knew? Knowing that would have helped explain a lot of things but the sad fact was I was never diagnosed or treated for ADD as a child. I'm not sure my parents recognized that there was something wrong, or maybe they just didn't want to accept the fact that there was. My Dad never liked school either, so they might have thought it was just another thing he and I had in common.

School was always an up and down adventure. For the first and second grade I was in Catholic School and "Sister's" worst nightmare. Additionally, I was sent to another school for speech class because I stuttered. There was no speech class available in Catholic schools at that time.

When I was in third grade, we moved to the suburbs. I never really liked school; I just liked the attention I could draw. I played basketball, football and soccer. I hated to lose. That was the absolute worst for me. I had this "extra" need to be the best at everything and I was the kind of kid that never gave up; tenacity was my middle name. It was the whole do-it or-die mentality even back then. Looking back I can see that I was always an extremist. I was never satisfied and quickly moved on to the next thing. I still have that behavior somewhat, and I constantly have to remind myself to slow down.

I was popular and likable and had what I thought was a pretty normal life. But, now that all those trappings of a "good life" are gone, I've been able to discover that my most important possession all along had been me. Finding the real me and learning about the person I really was has been my biggest achievement. Too bad it took over 30 years and a prison term to learn it, but my incarceration was an extremely valuable learning tool and it has been a life-changing and life-saving event. With the path I was on, a prison term was almost pre-destined. At least now, I recognize that.

Additionally, I have to acknowledge that there were several childhood experiences that were detrimental to and major players in my development, or should I say my "mis-development."

Nick was my mother's father. His nickname was Buddy. I don't know where that nickname came from as he was anything but a "buddy" to anyone. The best thing I can say about him is he was the meanest man to ever walk the face of this earth. He was a loose cannon and I don't think

I spent one good moment with him. My brothers and I were the first grandchildren born into the family on my mother's side. One time my younger brother, Sal, messed his diaper when we were at Buddy's house. My brother was maybe two at the time. As a punishment, Buddy stripped him of his clothes and hit his butt hard with a stick. Then, without a stitch of clothing on, he locked him outside on the porch until my mother came to pick us up after work. Sal cried the entire day.

Buddy's famous saying was, "Up Mike's rear" (only he didn't use the word "rear"). My first memory of this was when I was three or four years old. It didn't matter what you asked for, that hurtful phrase was always his answer. I hated hearing that and to this day it still doesn't make any sense to me. As young as I may have been, I couldn't help but feel that it was a direct slam at me and I always felt like crying. Buddy was the first person I ever hated. No matter how hard I tried, I could *never* please him. As young as I was, I knew enough to answer, "No, Buddy, there's nothing up there."

We spent a lot of time with my maternal grandparents. Both my Mom and Dad worked. My mother worked in retail so it involved nights and weekends. My Dad worked all the time. We saw Buddy physically abuse our grandmother. If she went shopping and misplaced the receipt, he would hit her. If she "spoke out of turn," he would hit her. If dinner was a minute late, he would throw it all on the floor. It was terrible for us to see. The sickest part was everyone was afraid of Buddy. That is, everyone except for me. I learned how to make him mad. My older brother, Vito, was Buddy's favorite. I did my best to cause trouble so that I could get Vito into trouble. Then, I would run like Forest Gump. I would run like the wind and hide from Buddy. I ran from him most of my life. I actually learned how to run fast by running from Buddy. One day he came to our house to pick Vito up. Sal and I asked him where he was going. He said, "Disneyland." Of course, we said we wanted to go, too. But Buddy said, "No, just Vito." As young as I was, I knew someday I would get him for that and I would get him slowly and deliberately.

45

During high school, our house was the hangout after school. Friends would come over and we would play sports in our side yard. Every day at the same time, Buddy would show up. We were just kids enjoying ourselves after school and this crazy man would drive all over the front yard and try to chase us down with his car. It was the highlight of the day. We all got the greatest joy out of pulling his strings. We watched him act like Homer Simpson on crystal meth. He would curse and scream and we would laugh and laugh. So, I think I did get him, even if it was just a little bit.

How does a child ever learn about love, compassion, kindness and simple self-respect when he doesn't witness it? Was this how a man was supposed to behave, hurt women, treat children like dirt? I believe the person I eventually turned into was partly the result of how I was treated by Buddy. Learning to run from authority was a simple reality I learned early from him. Ironically, running from authority is what eventually sent me to prison. Buddy died from cancer and I hope before he died he had a minute of regret for some of the things he had done during his lifetime. When Buddy died, few tears were shed. His grave doesn't get visited very often and his name is rarely spoken. That's not the epitaph I want.

Then there was one morning in fall 1986. I was six years old. Every day my Dad would get up early for work. This morning was no different. He got up and so did I. I remember this morning so clearly. I started begging him to take me to work with him. Every day, the same thing would happen. I would beg to go to work with him and he would pick me up and put me into bed with my mother until it was time to get ready for school. He would say, "Don't worry, some day you will be able to run the business, but for now, you have to stay home and go to school." He would assure me that he would be home by six o'clock. I would give him a hug and kiss goodbye and say, "Okay, I will see you at six and I love you." He would tuck me into bed close to my mother. Then he would leave for work.

On this morning, it had been about 10 or 15 minutes after he had put me back in bed when I heard the sound of a breaking glass. I didn't get up because I figured that he had dropped his coffee cup or something. A minute later, I opened my eyes to see a six-foot tall man holding a big knife to my mother's throat. As he tried to wake her up, I hid under the covers and started to tap her on her side to wake her up. My mom was in a deep sleep until he yanked her out of bed. Once she was on her feet, he asked where all the money was. She told him there was no money in the house. Then he slapped her in the face and dropped her to the ground. My mother screamed. Then he said he wanted her purse. When she only had 25 cents, he was mad and he slapped her again. But, this time he dragged her down the hallway and downstairs. That's when I got out of bed and woke up my brothers and made them hide. Ironically, our "hiding place" was always in our parent's bedroom. I tried to call 911 but when I picked up the phone there was no dial tone. The guy must have cut the wires. I ran down the hallway looking for my mother. Sal followed me and when we got to the stairway, we inched our way down a few stairs and she must have heard us on the stairs because she yelled, "Get back upstairs!" When we got to the fourth step down, we could see this man holding the knife to my mother's throat as he raped her. We didn't know what it was called then, but that's what it was. Then we both ran back upstairs not knowing what to do. As he raped her, he beat her. Once he was done, he robbed our house.

My mother was on the couch unable to move. As soon as I heard him leave the house, I ran downstairs and told my mother that I was going next door to get help. Out the front door, I ran like the wind to the neighbor's house to call the police and my father.

The police were there in minutes and my father was there in seconds or so it seemed. Several of the officers knew my Dad because they had grown up together and were from the same neighborhood. I remember the K-9 dogs that came into the house. Once they finished inside, they went outside to begin their search for the guy. The dogs tracked him down just a couple of blocks from our house. He had gone back to his girlfriend's house. They found his clothes in a refrigerator and they found him hiding naked under the sink. He was arrested and went to prison for 15 years.

My mother was badly beaten. She needed stitches on her mouth and was tested for HIV and AIDS. My mother's bruises lasted a long time but the memory of that day has lasted a lifetime. God bless my Mom, because she survived a terrible event. I love her with all my heart. When it happened, I was mad, really mad and scared but she showed me how strong one had to be to overcome the obstacles that can come your way. I think that experience is what stole away my trust for others.

No matter how much time passes, that morning remains as vivid as if it happened yesterday. Neither my mother nor I ever went for counseling after that happened. And, to this day, I don't know why. I have wondered about it for all these years. Maybe my parents thought I was just too young to remember. But, I remember.

I've had over five years to take a really hard look back at my life. I started to see how my life's chain of events played out and what the results were. I was always in trouble at school. I had no respect for anyone, least of all teachers. I feared nothing. I got bounced between high schools because my behavior was so bad. I had so much anger and disrespect towards elders. Eventually, I was shipped to a school 45 minutes outside of the district in order for me to go to school at all. I got kicked out of that one, too. My parents put pressure on the home district and they took me back but with a million rules and restrictions. Of course, it was only a matter of time before I broke those rules, too. School was fun for all the wrong reasons. I don't know how I learned anything. I graduated but only by the skin of my teeth.

None of the kids I knew or looked up to were "college bound." I saw no reason to continue going to school. I had a ready-made job waiting for me. I had a great family business and I was going to run it with my Dad. Who needed school? Not me. My entire outlook on life was so messed up. Everything I did, I did for the wrong reasons. I had friends and I belonged to the cool group. But I really was just a clown back then. I was never a person who made things easy. I did the complete opposite from everyone else. I never learned the lesson when the lesson was taught. The value system I developed was based solely on superficiality. I had no depth of character, and the word "integrity" was not in my vocabulary.

At 16, I was able to buy a car not because I *deserved* a car, but because I wanted one. Although it wasn't a new car, it was a car and I loved her. Well, I loved her at first. I took such good care of her, waxed her and kept her clean and beautiful. My car was a candy apple red hatchback that had a nice little sound system in it. I thought I was the coolest kid in town until one day my friends and I pulled up to a red light and ended up next to a full-size Bronco. He almost blew out my car windows from the bass that was coming out of his system. I saw red. I drove directly to a local sound shop and ordered the loudest car system in town.

The car was in the shop for a week and a half. Every time my parents asked about the car, I told them it was in the shop getting fixed. I'm sure they knew I was up to something but they had no idea what. To make a long story short, when the car was done, I called my Dad and asked him to meet me at the shop. He was stunned to see the $3,600 bill. My Dad was so mad at me, and he had every right to be. But, when he saw how happy and excited I was, he paid the bill without hesitation. I was not only a lost child, but I was an exceptionally spoiled, lost child with a value system based on possessions.

I think all three of us were spoiled because my father tried to make up for the way Buddy treated us. Especially with the difference in the way he treated Vito compared to Sal and me. I think my Dad knew what Buddy did to us, but I don't think he knew what to do about it. I think he decided that he would make up for Buddy's mistreatment of us by giving us anything we ever wanted. I grew up with an *extraordinary* need to be loved and accepted. I guess I thought *things* gave me that acceptance. Everything was money and I learned how to get money any time I needed it. What I didn't realize was the only thing material possessions guaranteed were superficiality and the inability to judge which "things" actually had value and which did not. I never thought twice about buying things I couldn't afford. I had Dad and Dad was rich, or at least that is what I thought. The truth was Dad went without to make sure others always had. His heart was so much bigger than his pocket ever could have been. He never learned how to say, "No."

One of the greatest regrets of my life has been acknowledging the fact that it took me so long to learn how wrong and how ungrateful I had been. It is so embarrassing to realize how fortunate I was and how selfishly and spoiled I had behaved. My only hope is that my Dad can see the change in me and that he is proud of the person I've finally become.

Mom and Dad weren't perfect. Their life together was definitely not ideal. My brothers and I had an abundance of things, but what we seriously lacked was order, discipline and consequences. One thing I have learned is that loving someone doesn't mean you always say, "Yes." Sometimes love means you say, "No." Sometimes, you have to do what is right, not what is easy.

When I was a junior in high school, I came home one day and found my father home, too. He *never* came home from work early. My brothers had gotten home from school before me that day. They were in the bedroom with my Dad and they were crying. I noticed my father packing some bags. So I asked him if he was going on vacation. He asked Vito and Sal to leave the room, and then he closed the door so it was just him and I. My father told me that he was not going on vacation but he was leaving my mother. He had rented a small townhouse and he was moving. I said, "Really, that's nice, but what about the rest of us"? That's when he said, "Don't worry, kid, you could come with me if you want, but only you. Vito and Sal have to stay here with your mother." I don't remember even blinking an eye. I asked him how long I had to get ready. He said, "I'd like to be out of here in 10 minutes." I told him all I needed was five. Then, I went to pack, too.

That day, not only did my father leave my mother, but so did I. What was I supposed to do? My father was my best friend. What I find so totally unbelievable is that I never gave my mother's or brothers' feelings a second thought. I was simply taking care of me. I was blinded by my undying allegiance to my father and the color green in his pockets. It was years before my mother said anything to me about that day. It was one thing for my dad to leave; it was another that I left, too. When she finally spoke to me about that day, she told me that when she came home from work, she found my brothers sitting at the kitchen table crying and waiting for my dad and me to come back home. My decision-making skills had always been poor. I made decisions impulsively, and never took the time to actually think through anything. I never stopped long enough to look at the possible consequences of my actions. I was the poster child for Nike Air—Just Do It!

As much as my father was always a very hard worker and very good provider, he did destroy our family. I was never the same after we left. I don't think any of us recovered very well. My Mom took the break up really hard. She was devastated, but she is one strong woman. She came back stronger than ever. But, still, I will never forgive myself for leaving her and my brothers that day.

My father taught me the ropes of everything. I studied my Dad's moves. I mastered his habits. In his prime, he was a womanizer and a gambler. He was never faithful to anyone. Not to my Mom or any of his girlfriends except for Janet, my step-mom. Consequently, I have never been faithful either. I guess I never understood that faithfulness was a requirement for a lasting relationship.

He took me to my first underground gambling joint when I was six years old. I was in awe of the whole scene. I was fascinated by the smoky room, the tables, and all the people I was introduced to. Everyone had a nickname, but no last name. There were people with names like Tony Cold-Cuts and Joey Hollywood, etc. My God, I was living in a movie. I was much too young to understand that the "glitter" was just tarnish. How could I understand what I witnessed was illegal? It was wrong. I wonder, just wonder how much that whole time influenced my development? Why did wrong always seem right?

At 13, I mowed the grass for my father's girlfriend, while my mother was home cooking our dinner. I thought my relationship with my father was just the coolest thing in the world. He included me in everything. I craved that acceptance so badly. I wasn't able to tell the difference between how right things were from how wrong they were. I went along with him on everything and in return he bought me anything I wanted.

As you can see, as great as our family was in some aspects, there were some twisted parts, too. How does a kid separate all that out? How do you hang on to the valuable ideals and discard the rest of the junk? My father's family was as different from my Mom's as they could possibly be. My Dad's father was Luke, Papa Luke to all of us. He was the patriarch of our Italian heritage. I never knew my grandmother, Nancy, because she died before any of us were born. But from what people say, she was a beautiful and kind woman. In fact, most people say she was a saint for being married to Papa. Papa Luke couldn't have been more opposite from Buddy. For one thing, he died broke. Papa Luke loved betting on horses and Sunday football, both of which contributed to his financial problems. But, I have to admit that he was my favorite.

Our relationship, too, couldn't have been more different than mine with Buddy. The only time Papa Luke ever put his hand on me was in my front yard after I burned our house down. Yes, that's what I said, burned our house down almost to a crisp. It was an accident due to carelessness from a lighted cigarette. I didn't do it on purpose. But, while we were watching the fire department put out the fire, Papa tapped me on the shoulder and when I turned around he gave me the famous Tandoi Right Hook to my forehead and left the "T" impression from his ring.

Other than that I can't ever remember fighting with him, but I used to watch him and my father fight every day at work over dumb stuff. He worked into his 70s, pushing a plate tapper on the asphalt crew. Let me tell you, he was the best at it. In his day, he was a building contractor. He and my great grandfather, Vito, built a track of really nice homes on a street they named for the family. But, that was long before I was born. In fact, my Dad was only five years old when the track was built.

After Papa's first wife died, he remarried several times. His last wife, Marie, is the person I know as Grandma Marie. She was a good wife to Papa and very kind and loving to all of us.

Papa Luke died before I went to prison and before my Dad died. Good thing because if cancer didn't kill him, my father's death would have. Papa Luke basically died alone, even though most of the family was at his bedside when he died. He was so angry that he had cancer and bitter that his life had not turned out as he had expected; he alienated most of those who cared about him. Most of his friends had already died and I think he was just lonely. He made decisions according to what he wanted, not so much for what was best. Hmm, sounds familiar. But, you know, I still miss him and probably always will.

The picture of a person's life is painted by the day-to-day events of that life. For me, July 26, 2003 was a pivotal day that I will never forget. It was a terrifying day and it should have been enough to change my life right then and there, but of course, it didn't. It was, however, the beginning of the final spiral that would end in my prison sentence.

I was the first one in at my father's paving company because I had been up all night getting high with my best lady friend, Crack Cocaine. It was a Saturday morning and I had my father's workers coming in so we could do a side asphalt job I had sold earlier in the week. Before going into the shop, I went to the customer's house and said that I needed an advance so that I could buy the materials needed for his job. One of the workers was with me in my truck.

I got the customer's money and drove straight to the crack house not realizing that the customer had followed me all the way to the drug house. So, the truth was I never had any intention of paving this guy's driveway that morning. I got the money, spent the money, and now I was busted. I tried to manage my way out of the humiliation of getting busted by my father's customer. I thought I had talked my way out of this mess at least temporarily. So, I got back into my truck and we left. I found my way to a side street and we started to smoke the crack. Out of nowhere my phone starts ringing and ringing and ringing. My father must have called me 30 times before I answered the phone. When I did answer, I was in for it. He gave me five minutes to get back to the shop or else he was going to kill me. And he meant it! So, I swallowed my pride, if you can call it that because I didn't have any pride left. I was a scum bag, full blown piece of crap. I got back to the shop and to my great surprise, there was my father *and* his customer.

To make things right with his customer, my Dad ate the cost of this guy's whole driveway. But instead of having the crew help me, he made me empty the entire dump truck of asphalt by hand with a wheel barrow and shovel; going up-hill in 86 degree weather. And, to boot, I'm geeked out of my own skin. What happened was my Dad tried to make me pay for my wrong. He wasn't having it any more. He knew exactly what I was up to and to make matters worse, I knew I was breaking his heart. He had built the company from the ground up and his word was his honor. For me to steal from his customer was unthinkable in his mind. But I felt powerless to change. How could the son he loved so much be doing this to himself? How could this drug have so much control over his son's life that he would steal from everyone that loved him? How could this be? Well, it was possible because addiction had me wrapped around her finger. I'd do anything for that next blast. Anything!

So, after I got done with the driveway, my Dad fed me and then tried to talk sense into me. We went to one of our favorite Italian restaurants, Rocky's. We had tripe, Italian bread, salad with crumbly blue cheese dressing and a nice cold Pepsi. By the time the meal was over, I was able to con my father into giving me the balance of $225 from my pay check. That was just enough for me to get through yet another night with my lady, Miss Cocaine. I knew I stunk after being up for days and I had worked asphalt in the heat of the day. I stopped at the "spot," grabbed $125 worth of crack, went home, showered, got high and I was off.

I dressed the part of "Tony" Scarface Tandoi, my street name. I was in full role-playing gear. Black shiny army pants, black Miami-vice shirt open at the neck, black hat, black shoes, and black baseball gloves. To complete the picture I wore black sunglasses. I was pumped up, fired up, motivated and I was going to have fun that night. It was roughly 4:30 p.m. so I made my way over to Jefferson Avenue-- the one-way street. I call it that because once you entered the Avenue, there was no way back. It was by far the worst street in the city. It was where the devil lived and roamed free.

I pulled up to my "spot" and I bought an 8 ball. Then I noticed a lady friend of mine and asked her if she would like to hang out. I ended up taking her to the neighborhood farmer's market and offered to buy some fruit and vegetables for her family. She accepted the offer. I actually felt that I had done something good and believe it or not, I didn't get high while she was with me. After the market, I took her home and asked if she would like to hang out later. I really liked this girl. She was a sweet, innocent girl living in a horrible neighborhood from which escaping was impossible. I wanted to help her, but I couldn't help myself let alone anyone else. She got out of the truck and told me to come back around 9 p.m.

Once she got out of my truck she came over to my window to give me a kiss goodbye and that's when it happened. It was 5:35 p.m. I was shot five times at point blank range with a .38 caliber gun. The first shot blew out the passenger-side window of the truck. The second shot went through my wrist which was protecting my head. By the third, fourth and fifth shots the guy lost control and was firing ghetto style-- sideways. I guess that was lucky for me because he hit me three times in my leg and not any higher in my body. One shot broke my femur bone, the next entered and went through my body just missing my groin and the last shot traveled from one side of me to the other. Of the five shots fired, four hit me and two of those are still lodged inside of me. My body was on fire. Blood was everywhere.

The kid took off as I tried to get out of the truck, but my femur snapped and I collapsed. I looked up to scream for help, but no one was there. I suppose my friend ran for her life. If you've ever watched a "hood" movie, when someone gets shot people close their doors. Take it from me, it's not just in the movies. It is the absolute truth. I don't know how I did it, but I pulled myself up with every ounce of strength I still had. I was determined not to die on Jefferson Avenue and Hawley Street. I got in the truck and started it even though the truck was a manual shift. Along with the snapped femur bone I had a broken wrist and it was so hard to drive but I managed to get out on to Jefferson Ave. I was in front of a used car lot and I blocked traffic from both sides by parking the truck sideways in the middle of the road. Then I got out of the truck and lay on the pavement face up looking to the sky praying to God to save my life and to please send someone to help me. Someone must have called for an ambulance and I was taken to Strong Memorial Hospital.

At the hospital, I was covered in blood and close to death from so much blood loss. All my fancy clothes were cut off of me. All alone on the stretcher, my life was literally in the hands of that medical staff. I told the doctor that I was high enough to stay awake for days and begged him not to put me out. I was terrified that I would never wake up again. My Dad and stepmom were out for the night; and my Mom and stepdad were away at the Thousand Islands. The only person that could be reached was a close friend. He got the call and he contacted my parents. It seemed like everyone got there right away. I know that was impossible but that is how it seemed to me.

I was alive but now I had a new name—John Doe. The shooter had not been caught and my Dad was really worried that he might try to find me, so after the two-week hospital stay my Dad made arrangements for me to "hide out" for a while. Even my family members didn't know where I was. Leaving the hospital was really tough because I couldn't walk, feed, dress or do anything by myself. My Dad's office manager and "right arm" to all of us, Tammy, arranged for me to go to her parent's house on Conesus Lake to recuperate.

Granny and Jim rebuilt me and, for the rest of my life, I will be indebted to them. I was a baby all over again. They spoon-fed, showered, shaved and dressed me. I couldn't do anything for myself. I stayed out at the lake for a long time recovering. I spent my days watching Wheel of Fortune, Jeopardy, and NY Yankee games. I ate ice cream seven days a week. Homemade jam was something I had never had before, and it was so good. Their kindness to me was amazing. I was treated like royalty, and I was beginning to actually enjoy a drug-free life. Don't misunderstand. I am not making light of the situation. Recovery wasn't easy. It was painful, and it took a long time. I absolutely did not take what happened casually. However, what I hadn't ever acknowledged before this happened was the anguish and wear and tear I'd placed on my family. I had been too wrapped up in myself and only concerned about when I could get high again.

The cost to my family was enormous. I don't mean just financially. The real cost was in the emotional stress of the shooting. What must it have been like for a parent, a brother, an aunt, a cousin who loved me, to face the fact that I was as close to death as I could have been at 23 years old? How many tears had they shed because of me? How many sleepless nights had they spent? I can't imagine ever getting a phone call from a hospital telling me my child had been shot and was on the verge of death. I don't have children yet, but I can only imagine the terror it must be for a parent.

While in the hospital, I was blessed with a wonderful and supportive caseworker who was able to help me get insurance and a treatment plan so that I could go to Conifer Park in Schenectady, NY. That is where I went after I was well enough to leave the lake. Conifer was a life-saving drug rehab program for me, at that time. I did well in the treatment program but truthfully, when I came home, I may have been off drugs but I was never really totally clean because I was still drinking. Sadly, after all of this, one year later I relapsed after an argument with my girlfriend and I bought another bag of crack on the same street where I had been shot!

The years 2001 to 2003 were a blur. In 2001, I opened a night club in downtown Rochester. Club NRG (like energy) was a huge success. The City of Rochester was looking for businesses to bring life back to the downtown area of the city and the club became the place to go. The first six months of business was phenomenal because I ran it like a business. I was 21 years old earning big money, really big money. Being me, I wasn't satisfied with a great business; it had to be over the top. Eventually, I held after-hours parties that lasted all night long. There was an open bar and every drug imaginable was available. The weekend coke parties started small but always ended really big. I was snorting a ton of coke by this time. I was on top of the world but the world was about to drop out from under me.

It was 9 p.m. on Friday night and I was getting the club ready for takeoff. I worked day and night, everyday. Even at 21 you can't do that for too long without paying the consequences. I decided to "start my engine" with a blast of coke—like usual. But this time, my nose started to burn like it was on fire. My nose "popped" and then "dropped." I lost one side of my passage way and my nose started to bleed and it would not stop. I was tearing up from the pain. I called my father and said, "Dad, I'm sorry to bother you, but I can't run the club tonight can you please come over and bail me out"? I told him what had happened. Long story short, he came over.

I went home and went to bed with a box of Kleenex. I slept from Friday night until Monday morning. I was still living with my Dad and I'm sure he checked on me to make sure I was still alive. But, I have no memory of that. By Monday morning when I woke up, I was extremely weak, in pain and stuck in the fetal position. I couldn't even open my hands. I was in the over-dosed drug-addicted body position. For those that don't know (and I hope you don't), the body goes into a paralyzed and helpless position. The only way out is to get high again. That is why most addicts save a little for mornings. When I was able to roll over to my nightstand, I found a little coke left on the glass. But, I wasn't able to get any of the coke because I was congested and my nose was closed up with dried blood. What a pathetic sight I must have been. Friday night I lost a nostril, my sheets, pillowcases, and bed were covered in dry blood and I smelled like a New York City sewer. Yet, I still wanted to try to sniff a line of coke.

I dragged myself out of bed and went to get some cereal. I remember the cereal so clearly because my father called me on the phone later in the day to yell at me for being a disrespectful slob. I had been so weak that I couldn't even pour the milk into the bowl and it went all over the counter. Of course, I left the mess.

Drugs and alcohol had such a grip on me that I had lost all control over my ability to live without them. It took about an hour before I was able to focus enough to take a shower and attempt to get to my father's shop. I went out to my car but it would not start. I never turned off the lights from Friday night so the battery was dead.

I couldn't call my Dad because he was doing a job 45 minutes out of town. The only option I had was to ride the motorcycle, a CBR650 crotch rocket. That was a really bad option, but I only had $500 in cash on me and I knew that wasn't enough. I had to get more cash so that I could get more drugs and this was the only way it was going to happen. Again, this would be another one of those life-changing decisions that would be disastrous in the end.

I was on the expressway and my body ached for drugs. Now that I couldn't use my nose to snort coke, what was I going to do? All I could think was, "Well you better figure something out." Instead of going straight off the expressway and into my father's shop, I turned right and drove to the inner city in search of a drug I didn't have to sniff. I drove down the streets until I found what I needed.

There I saw a guy wearing a NBA jacket with all the team names listed on it. I rode over to him and said, "I think you're the guy I'm looking for. I've never bought crack before so I don't know how to do this." I asked for $200 worth. He and the guys with him wanted to know if I was a cop. I assured them I wasn't and told them my sad story and they believed me.

I rode off to find a bodega shop to buy the essentials I needed to smoke the crack. I made my way to a park and found a grassy area. Mind you, I had never smoked this stuff before and I was completely new at it. I managed to pack the stem. I lit it and began to inhale and didn't stop until my body was completely filled with smoke. I held in the smoke as long as I could and slowly began to exhale and as I did my entire world changed.

Right then and there, I was hooked! I saw the sky and everything around me change. I had crossed over into the devil's playground and now he was in control. Before the stem had even cooled down, I was back on the bike looking for the dealer again.

That's all it took to make my life go from bad to much, much worse. My life, as I knew it, ended that day. I had new priorities, a new purpose. The more I got high the worse I became. That very first blast lasted six months. I never stopped. Nothing would get in my way. I was on a self-destructive path and it was this period of time that caused the most pain and humiliation to me and my family. My drug use caused my dreams to dissolve into thin air. I ruined everyone around me. If I knew you while I was getting high, you probably were getting high, too. Because of my bad influence, my brothers, best friends and the people that worked for me all started using crack.

As a kid, my favorite movie of all time was *A Bronx Tale*. I *loved* that movie. It was an American crime drama that followed a young Italian-American teenager, Cologero Agnello, as his path in life was guided by two father figures. One was his father, Lorenzo Agnello, and the other was a local Mafia boss, Sonny "Three Fingers." I must have watched that movie, easily, a hundred times and each time I would learn something new. There was one lesson that I should have learned but chose not to because, just like Cologero ("C"), I was too young to understand. In one scene, "C" was starring out the window fantasizing about the "gangster" life—the fast life with all its fame, wealth and power. His father said to him, "Son, there is nothing worse in life than wasted talent. Right now you are too young to understand but one day you will." I wish I had been able to understand then, but I, too, was too young. You see, I was desperately chasing that life. I wanted to be the next "Sonny" no matter what the cost. At that point of my life I only valued material things. I had ability, but what I lacked was the maturity to handle it.

The entire first part of my life was wasted. The potential I had for success was truly unlimited. When I graduated from high school, my father said to me, "Michael, what do you want to do now? Would you like to go to college or do you want to start your own seal coating business"? "I want my own business, Dad," I replied without hesitation. That was when I was 17 years old. By the time I was 19 years old, I was in competition for every major seal coating job in Rochester. I didn't get every job, but I didn't miss a bid. My father and I called sealer "Black Gold." If I had only operated that business like a real business, today I would be a very wealthy man and, most importantly, one without a prison record. But I was just too young and too hungry for the all the wrong things.

Club NRG was packed each weekend and most week nights. I had the best sound system, the best lighting and best promoter. I had the best entertainment in town. I built the club with my own hands and I hand-picked the people who worked for me. The money that was coming in was beyond anything even I could imagine. I know you've heard the saying, "It's too good to be true." Well, I am here to tell you, it's the truest statement ever spoken. I remember the day my father told me that the club business was the "curse" that destroyed our family. The look on his face and the sadness in his voice was more than I could bear. That club was too much of a success and I was too young to handle it. It was too much money and power for me because I was still a young punk kid with too little understanding of which things really mattered in life.

Once I was on crack, I lived my life only for the next blast. It wasn't very long before the drug abuse took over my life. My state of mind could only be described as extreme paranoia. I was convinced I was being followed by invisible people. They lived in the walls. I wish you could understand how terrified I was all the time. Me, Michael, the one who was never afraid of anything was now scared stiff. There were times that I would answer the door of the club with a shotgun in my hand because I needed it to chase away the invisible people. Staff would arrive for work and they would call out to me, "Mike, Mike" only to find me hiding in the ceiling tiles. Once I knocked down an entire wall with a jackhammer because I was convinced that there were people living in the wall. There was even a day that I chased down a Lift-line Van because I thought it was transporting aliens.

My dealers were giving me a line of credit that could have supported a small city. I had a weekly habit that ran between $7000 and $12,000. My drug life overtook everything. My Dad was devastated. He tried everything to make me see how deeply I had sunk. Then, I lost the club. It was my pride and joy—gone! I built it with my own hands. I was happier and more successful than I had ever been. How did it go so fast? I had reduced myself to stealing every bottle of liquor I had so that I could trade it off with the dealers. I broke open the pay phones and arcade games, anything that had money so that I could cash it in with the dealers. If it wasn't bolted down, I took it; even when it was bolted, I figured out how to get what I needed.

It was at this point that I began to accept that I was in way over my head and I was in really bad shape. It was time for me to go back to rehab. I checked myself into Conifer Park Rehab Center for a 31-day program. I honestly thought this was going to be it. This time would change my life. I wanted so badly to dig myself out of the hole I had dug for myself.

After the Conifer program ended, I came home and went back to work. At first, I felt that I had found some peacefulness in my life. But, as time went on my workload increased. Now I was working three jobs; the asphalt business with my father, my own seal coating business and additionally, I started another business. I bought a pontoon boat that I overhauled to be a floating hot dog stand. With the help of my girlfriend, we sold lunch and dinner options to boaters and people along the shore of Lake Ontario. It was an amazing idea and tremendously successful but, at the same time, immensely stressful. There was no time for sleeping, no time for me. I became the hamster on a wheel. I just kept working, working and working. The obsession with the "go big or stay home" mentality had taken over my life once again. I could feel that things were slipping away. Everything seemed right but then again, nothing was right and slowly I returned to what I knew best—drugs. How did I let this happen again?

CHAPTER 3

True Darkness

THERE IS A SAYING IN drug rehab that you start back right where you left off in your drug addiction. Believe me when I tell you it's a fact. This is when I entered the darkest part of my life. I was now on a three-week crack binge. It was non-stop crack smoking. Up all day, up all night. It was one of those self-inflicted crack cocaine suicide missions led by the Devil himself.

I hallucinated constantly. I was extremely paranoid; convinced I was being pursued by Special Forces. I was trapped in a terrifying world that only existed for those who foolishly chose to enter. All I can say is it was real to me.

One day in 2006, I was in my 1992 Chevy Corvette, smoking crack and running for my life from imaginary police. I was convinced that I was being chased by invisible demons from the dark side and a Special Forces Unit that wanted to recruit me for a secret operations' program. I was doing at least 100 mph on the expressway. I was driving for my life. I was in a high-speed run for freedom. I got off of the expressway and ended up in a suburb of Rochester called Rush-Henrietta. I wasn't familiar with this area and I was amazed that the road was surrounded by farmland with no stop lights and long straight-aways. I felt lucky that the road was like that. I could really open up the Corvette and escape my imaginary foes. I torched the wick on my crack pipe and put my foot down on the gas pedal. I lost control of the car and it started spinning in circles and ended up in a cornfield. Instead of simply backing up and getting back on the road, my mind was telling me that this was the perfect hiding place from the cops, the demons and the special unit that were all hunting me down. So, I drove through the cornfield with my beautiful Corvette. I hit ruts, bottomed out and tore through the corn stalks and plowed through the field trying to protect myself from the imaginary villains.

I noticed that on the outer edge of the field there was a wide grassy path that was smoother than the field. So I began to make my way over to the path thinking it would be easier for me to drive the car there. It was a beautiful day, 80 degrees and sunny. As I rode the outer edge of the cornfield, I noticed another patch of grass that was shaped like a driveway and I thought it would be the perfect spot to park my car. By this time the radiator was bubbling with fluid and the spark plugs were misfiring. At that point, the car didn't sound too healthy so I decided it would be a good time to let the car cool down and, besides, I was bugging out!

I smoked some more crack and then I got out of the car and noticed a wooded area that reminded me of the wilderness of the Amazon. I have never been to the Amazon, but I was positive this was how it looked. Trees had long vines hanging from the branches. I was drawn to this area by a "force" which told me to enter. As soon as I crossed from the grassy path in the cornfield to the wooded area, life changed again. A voice was telling me that this was a challenge course and I had to pass through it in order to continue with the special operation program. I "understood" that the vines on the trees represented Challenge #1 and I was supposed to climb the vines and swing from tree to tree like a monkey. Well, I failed at swinging from tree to tree. In fact, I fell flat on my face. I got up and started to walk deeper into the woods. That's when I saw the castle. The voice told me there was a princess living there that needed to be rescued and it was my job to save her. But before I could save her I would have to cross the creek, Black Creek.

I took a break and another monster hit of crack. I took a blast that rivaled a NASA liftoff. I knew I needed to undress so that I wouldn't get my clothes wet, but more importantly, I didn't want the water to ruin my crack. In Challenge #2, I was supposed to walk across the water on the logs that were submerged in the water. What I didn't know was the logs were very slippery. Every time I tried to walk across the logs I fell flat on my face. It hurt so much, but I kept trying until the voice told me that I failed so now I would have to swim across like a frog. Now the creek wasn't very deep maybe four feet at the deepest point and I was scraping my whole body on the rocks that must have been in this creek forever.

I was exhausted and I had no idea how long I'd been trying to cross the creek. It could have been hours. Time stands still. So I decided that I would go back to the bank, smoke more crack and rest. As I reached the bank, I collapsed from exhaustion. I struggled to repack the stem and managed to take another hit. This time I woke up the Devil in full force and he started talking to me. His voice was booming, very deep and very powerful. He said, "Michael, take a good look around you. If you stay here with me, I will provide you with all the crack you will ever want." At that point, all the rocks in the water turned to crack rocks. Everywhere I looked there was crack cocaine. In my mind, I questioned how I would be able to smoke that crack since my stem was just about gone. I didn't say it out loud, I just thought it. The Devil said, "Don't worry, Michael, I will give you all the stems there are in the world." At that moment, all the wood that was floating in the creek turned to stems. The creek was full of stems and they were all headed down stream. I remember feeling scared--terrified was more like it. My mind was racing; my thoughts were scattered. Then the Devil said, "So what's it going to be, Michael? Are you going to join my team or what?"

I was either soaking wet from the water or dripping wet from sweat. I was totally naked. Without hesitating for a minute, I jumped up and said to the Devil, "I'm with God; I don't want your stems. I don't want anything to do with you or your world." I started yelling out to God to save my life. I heard God say to me, "Run, Michael, run." And I followed what He said to do. I ran and ran. I ran through some thorny branches and I ran through the wooded area in circles until I found my car. I left behind all my clothes, my money, and the crack. I left everything I had in the world.

Thank God, the keys were still in the ignition. I don't know what would have happened if they hadn't been left in the car. That's the day I truly understood what fear was and I longed to be out of the darkness. I could actually feel the light of Christ guiding me. I started the engine and took off. I was flying along the grassy path that ran next to the monstrous cornfield. I was driving so fast I almost lost control of the car several times. That's when I saw the barn! There was a huge barn next to a huge house. I decided that I would try to tip my car sideways, on two wheels, so that I could slip into the barn. Then, at that moment, the light on the dashboard clicked on and I had to slam on the brakes. My car was smoking and the temperature gauge was past the red zone. I knew I had to get out of the car. Remember, I am totally naked. I started running down the driveway in the middle of nowhere. I didn't have any idea where I actually was. As I ran down the driveway, an SUV was heading toward me. I continued running until I was at the driver's window. The driver had to have known that I was in a panic because I was crying and screaming. In fact, I was hysterical.

He very calmly told me to back away from his SUV. He must have seen my car because he told me to go back to my car and wait for him. When you are under the influence of drugs, paranoia is rampant. You cannot clearly understand anything and you cannot trust what you think you see because you don't know what is real and what isn't. At that point, I was convinced that he was going to call the police and I could not go to jail then, I just couldn't. I was in total distress and said to him, "Sir, please I am all messed up on crack. The Devil just attacked me and God told me to run. So here I am. Please don't call the cops, please, Sir, call my Dad."

That is exactly what he did, he called my Dad. The man that God had me run to was a 25-year recovering addict. After he called my Dad, he took me into his house and gave me some of his clothes to wear and the most wonderful glass of orange juice I ever drank in my life. I was scratched and bruised from head to foot but I was safe and protected from my demons in this stranger's home. My father and girlfriend were there to claim me in about 30 minutes.

I made a very real choice that day—light or darkness, life or death and I chose light. I chose God. I ran for the Lord like I'd never run before. The man kept my car for a week and fixed it so I could drive it. He returned all of the belongings I left behind except for the drugs. I didn't ask for the drugs because I didn't want them. When I got home I slept for two days and stayed clean for the next three.

I was never a "religious" person. We didn't go to Church every Sunday but I had always been a spiritual person. I had talked to God my whole life. Of course, it was always to ask for something, but even then I knew there was a greater Being. As much as I truly believed that He had saved me that day, I wasn't strong enough to stay away from crack. There would be one more relapse. That incident would be the precursor to the day that would lead me straight to prison.

I was now on another five-week binge and there was one cop in particular who had been harassing me for a while. He called my cell phone to tell me he wanted to arrest me that day. I told him good luck and I'll see you in court tomorrow. I was forever the punk and I feared nothing (except for "aliens"). I already had a court date set for the next day for some nonsense warrant this particular cop took over a month to produce. I hung the phone up and realized that I was a wanted man. The writing was on the wall. But, I was determined not to let that spoil my day.

I had enough crack and money to last one more day. I was with my girlfriend and we would have the day together until 2:30 p.m. when we would pick her children up from school. The day went something like this. We dropped the kids off at school at 7:30 a.m.; I went to buy a $250 crack supply; changed a flat tire on my girlfriend's car; got the phone call from the cop; and met my girlfriend at a house we were considering buying.

I had one other stop to make that day before I headed home. I drove to the rehab center I attended as part of my current probation to speak with my caseworker. I asked if she would call my probation officer to tell him I would not be able to attend our scheduled meeting. I told her that I was going to check into the center for rehab because I realized that I needed help and I knew I was running out of time. I was going to die out on the street if I didn't get help. All of that was a story to stall for time, but on some level there was a lot of truth because throughout my time of addiction my body usually shut down after about five weeks of constant drug use and I would end up in bed for a few days. So, this was my stalling mechanism. She saw that I was in trouble and as I left, she actually ran after me to try to stop me from driving. The probation officer did clear me from that appointment.

With my probation officer out of the way, my plan was to get high and nothing was going to stop me. I met up with my girlfriend and we picked her kids up from school. We changed cars—I had her car because I had fixed her tire and she had mine. Her 8-year-old daughter came with me and her 10-year-old son rode with her. You have to understand, I loved those kids like they were my very own. I would have done anything for them. But at that moment in time, I couldn't do anything for anyone. As luck would have it, my girlfriend got into an accident right after we changed cars. I knew that the police would be on their way so I had to get as far away from the accident scene as I could. The police showed up and put my girlfriend and her son in the back of the police cruiser. I had left with her daughter and headed for home. The whole time I was "geeking" like crazy. When that happens I cannot control the movements of my body. I was twitching and moving a mile a second. Yes, I was high and drove with a child in the car. My girlfriend's daughter was like my own daughter. We had a wonderful relationship and I told her that I needed help and that I loved her with all my heart. Even at 8 years old, she could see that I needed help and she loved me so much all she wanted was for me to stay alive. As we were reaching the house, I noticed there were cops in the neighborhood and it seemed to me that they were "in waiting" at the house. Some of that notion was imagined, but a lot was factual.

So, I dropped her off at a neighbor's house down the street from our house. She didn't want to leave. She begged me to stay with her but I was determined to keep on the run. In my highly paranoid state, this was war and I wasn't going to give up or go into hiding. But, even in my paranoia, I knew I had to protect her and keep her safe. She could not be in the car with me. As she got out of the car, I spotted the cop who had been out to get me for all those months. He and I made eye contact… and the race was on.

Our car doors passed side to side with no room to open the door. This was a "let's get high" suicide run. I was a man with an out-of-control mission. I had everything to lose but was much too stupid to consider the potential outcome. I drove straight for the expressway so that I could open up and outrun the cops.

My Dad had gone to help my girlfriend at the accident. By time he got to the accident scene, my name could be heard over the police radios as the call went out for all available cars to assist in a high-speed chase. My father called me on the phone but I told him I didn't have time. I was in a high-speed chase. Click, I hung up. Then the cop calls me, "Tandoi, just pull over." Click, I hung up. Then I smoked more crack.

I drove through two more towns and I figured that the best thing to do was to get off the expressway. I was going to take the next exit when I noticed the steel spikes on the ground and the road block. That is when it happened! I slammed on my brakes and took a turn that would change my life forever. I went down the grassy hill to avoid the steel spikes and when I hit the road again, my car crashed and bounced the wrong way on the expressway.

Cars were coming at me and I was in the middle lane trying to dodge them. I didn't want to hurt anyone and I don't think I wanted to die but now I was scared—so, so scared. I drove as far away from traffic as possible and found my way over to the middle, grassy patch so I could go wild in the grass and still be away from on-coming traffic. I was clocked at 120 mph. Cops were everywhere; behind me, in front of me. I was surrounded by cop cars. I was running out of grass and there was a bridge ahead so I had to get back on the road going the wrong way. I was hugging the guard rail and I didn't want to crash and I didn't want anyone to get hurt. I was running because I didn't trust the cops. In my state of mind, I thought everyone was after me. I wasn't going to stop—I couldn't stop, I had to keep going.

Sparks were flying because the passenger side of my car was scraping the rail. Then, I hit a car, head on. Both of the cars exploded, my airbag went off and I went into a deep panic. I tried to keep going. I didn't want to stop. I grabbed my crack stem and started to take a hit and kept hitting until the cops surrounded my car with guns drawn.

Cops were everywhere, guns were everywhere, and television news crews were everywhere. Looking back, I have to say that the news crews probably saved my life that day because I think the cops would have kicked my rear all over the expressway. They had been after me for so long. They wanted me so badly. In the police report, one cop wrote, "As I passed him, his window was down and it felt like the life was sucked right out of him—we were that close, window to window-- suction."

I kept smoking crack until one of the cops reached in and threw my crack stem out. He grabbed it from my mouth and burned his hand as he tossed it out of the car. The cops had me face down yelling the standard "stop resisting" so that they could roughhouse me legally. I had to wait for the ambulance to come because I was in bad shape. I was covered in blood and sweat. I was soaked. The victim was a 19-year-old young man. I thank God every day that he survived, but at the time he was so mad that we collided, all he wanted to do was physically fight with me. The cops had to order separate ambulances because he was so angry.

I was transported to the hospital and I stayed there for three days. I had a minor concussion but played it as long as I could. Within the first two hours at the hospital, the judge and the cops came to place me under arrest and to tell me a $50,000 bail had been set. My attorney was also present. My family showed up but I was cuffed down. It was lights out! Three days later, I got transported to the county jail and I couldn't get bail because my probation office had "red tagged" my case. This was it, the final act that would send me to prison for a long time.

I don't plan to have another day like that ever again and I won't as long as I stay drug and alcohol free. Looking back now, I can't believe it ever happened. I can't imagine that I was capable of doing something like that. To know that I allowed crack cocaine to control of my life is a very sobering realization. Thinking back to that day, I wonder how my Dad felt hearing my name over a police radio. How much did he fear for my life knowing I was in a high-speed chase and under the influence of drugs? How terrible it must have been to know he couldn't do anything—that he couldn't protect me from me?

What I do know now is with drugs in my life, I'm nobody, and incarceration is the only avenue for me. However, as long as I do the right thing, act like a man and live a life of recovery, my family and I will never have to experience my destructive behavior ever again. Sadly, but truthfully, I have to admit the judge was right. I was not only a danger to myself, but I *was* a danger to society.

CHAPTER 4

Turning the Corner

THE CAR CHASE AND ITS aftermath is what finally landed me in prison. It still took a number of years before I actually hit bottom. When I had nowhere else to go and I couldn't find another wall to hit, I knew it was time for a change. However, I still had no idea what that meant. I knew nothing about recovery or change; I knew nothing about who I was or how I felt. I couldn't even identify how I wanted to feel. I'd been under a spell for so many years that I just got accustomed to living on the dark side of life.

The last night in the box, when I got down on my knees to pray to God to help me with the extortion charge, I never in a million years could have predicted all that would happen to me. Unfortunately, I was one of those people who had to learn things the hard way or should I say, learn in the hardest way. But, learn I did. Looking back now, I understand how deeply I had strayed and how disrespectful of myself and everyone else I had become. I finally began to feel the pain from my mistakes and the bad choices I had made. I actually ached inside because I now could recognize how much God truly had blessed me from the very beginning of my life, yet I had never stopped long enough to recognize the gift. I took advantage of everyone and everything. I selected every wrong road in my fanatical quest for acceptance.

But before that night, when I prayed to God to save me, those concepts had never occurred to me. The only way I can explain my former life is to say that those were the blind years. Love was unknown to me because I never took the time to learn how to love and respect myself first. Michael got lost because he was too busy reaching for the next shiny object.

So, once the Captain cleared me of the extortion charge, I made a concentrated effort to change my life. I decided that one way to change would be for me to get a different job. I had lost my job with the grounds crew so I went to the C.O. in charge of the paint crew. I had known him for a while and he was an awesome, standup guy. I explained that I really needed to get out from under the radar scope and stay low keyed. He gave me a job.

I liked working on the paint crew. I worked with six other inmates and we would paint all day whatever needed to be painted. I was by far the messiest painter of the group. On the crew, there was a guy named Gill, whose buttons we could push so easily. He loved to talk about the corruption in the NYC police department. When we got him going there was no way of turning him off. It really made the day go by fast. My boss was the absolute best! I don't know why, but he reminded me of my father. He had a "big-shot" attitude and you could tell he loved women.

One afternoon I was painting the railings on the outside of Building 3 where all the counselors worked. One of the counselors came out and I said, "Hey, you're the drug lady." She replied, "Yes, I am. My name is Ms. DiBraccio." She was in charge of the ASAT program at Mid-State. ASAT stands for Alcohol and Substance Abuse Treatment Program. I started asking her questions about the program. I told her that I had just finished Small Engine Trade School but all I could seem to do was think about using drugs again. I added that I thought I needed some recovery in my life because up to now I had been living all wrong and I wanted to try something new. Then I asked if she could help me out. She told me to write her a letter requesting to be added to the program. She said, "Don't get high and I'll see what I can do." She did get me into the program but at that time, my counselor was Mr. Ferraro. At one of our meetings he said to me, "Tandoi, I don't like you, I don't like anything about you and I especially don't like that you are in this program. You give me one reason to kick you out and I will make sure you are out of here." You see, I really didn't qualify to take any of the treatment programs because I had so much time left on my sentence. I knew that even before I asked Ms. D about the program. Ordinarily, inmates start this program when they are one year away from their earliest release date. I had four years left, but I lied when I told her that I felt like I wanted to use again. That wasn't the truth, I didn't want to use again, but I was still working in my old style "maneuvering" my way into getting what I wanted. The real reason why I wanted to get into the program was that my friends were in the program. I wanted to be with them. But, from the day I began, I was wide-eyed and open to the new environment. There were so many opportunities within this program. I found that I was excited just to get started. Did I know what I was getting myself into? Absolutely not! But so many things just started to fall into place. I can honestly say this was the very beginning of my re-birth and my path to recovery. At the end, the real Michael would finally emerge. Even Mr. Ferraro was surprised and we actually had the opportunity to build a trusting relationship.

ASAT is a six- to nine- month program depending on your situation. It was all new to me and I had no idea where it could take me but, for the first time, I actually realized how fortunate I was to be in any program. After living so long for all the wrong reasons, I decided it was time for a change. I decided that I would try living for all the right reasons. This was the beginning of my struggle to learn about me, my addiction and how my childhood experiences contributed to my destructive behavior.

I started to search for something I wasn't able to describe but knew was missing from my life. So many times I had failed to take a realistic look at life. I didn't really know anything about life. I thought I had been living the dream life. Didn't I have it all? Didn't I have every material possession a person could want? If all those things were important and vital for happiness, why, then, had true happiness eluded me? No, there had to be something else. For the first time I wanted to know where was honesty and integrity? Where was love, where was satisfaction and contentment? Where was my self-respect?

Setting out to find where I left my self-respect has been one of the hardest and most challenging journeys I've had to take. I don't know when I last remember having self-respect. The fact that the word starts with "self" made me re-adjust my thinking. Getting reacquainted with me took time. I guess you could say that I forgot who I was. Was I really Mike Tandoi the crack head, or Mike Tandoi the local tough guy? Was I really nothing more than an unfaithful, lying, stealing, disrespectful spoiled child or was I someone greater than that? Did I have a purpose in life, and if so, what was that purpose?

Just like a scene from *A Bronx Tale*, I remember the day my father sat me down and said, "Michael, before you die you'll be able to count your true friends on one hand." I remember looking at him like he had two heads or had lost his mind. I said, "Dad, I have so many friends I need to borrow your hands and the hands of 50 others to count them all." They say you are who your friends are. And, that was what I had to change. Don't get me wrong, in prison you don't really make friends, you make a lot of acquaintances. If you're lucky enough or blessed enough you might be able to add one or two guys to your fingers.

One of the best things incarceration taught me was how to be a true friend. It took me a long time to open my heart so that I could receive the part of life called "friendship." Friendships and relationships take a lot of trust. Trust is hard to come by in prison. But even in a place of lost faith, friendship is possible. It was at Mid-State where I met a guy who, if I had a million years, would never have expected that we would become friends. Craig is the most genuine man I have had the blessing to know. He was a religious man and a bad guy who sought a new way of life. On the outside, we had very little in common. For one thing, Craig was a Black, African-American and Muslim. I was Caucasian, Italian-American, and Catholic but on the inside we were so similar. He taught me how to accept a person unconditionally. Craig was instantly a part of my life in prison but I didn't even know it. Craig and I had one big thing in common; we both felt deep pain caused by the demons of crack cocaine. We had both experienced similar feelings, mentally and physically. We both had corrupt pasts, and had hit rock bottom. Both of us had nowhere else to turn. At Mid-State, when one of us fell, the other was somehow always there to help him back up. There were times when Craig would barricade himself into his living area and go for days without talking to people and we just "accepted it." Why did he do that? It wasn't because he was angry or acting out, it was because he was meditating and praying to his God. Craig was the most inspirational guy I have ever met. As different as we were, we somehow bonded and learned to trust each other. I think we bonded because we both had the same destination—recovery! It was a hard-fought journey. I remember the day that Craig received a letter from his daughter and he asked if I wanted to read it. Any correspondence from family is precious and very private. Since he offered the letter to me I said, "Sure." I wasn't prepared for what I read. Craig had committed a serious offense and he had been away from home for quite awhile. His daughter was now 12 years old. If I didn't know that, I would have thought she was much older judging from her letter. She wrote a very honest letter. She told her father that she did not want to visit him in jail. Her P.S. said it all. "I'm praying and have never and will never stop, but you can't quit either." I looked at his face and I could almost hear his heart breaking. I was very fortunate that we traveled that same road together. Craig left Mid-State in 2011 and hasn't come back!

So, just like "C", from the movie, *A Bronx Tale*, I began to understand what my father was trying to teach me. I can tell you now, that I can count my true friends on one hand. There is sadness in that knowledge because I had to come to prison to learn that lesson. How I wish my Dad were here so that I could tell him that he was right. Why couldn't I have learned it sooner and under better circumstances? Why didn't I realize that people that use you aren't really friends? But then again, why did I think I was such a good friend? Didn't I use people, too?

Within two weeks of starting the ASAT program, I was offered a detail supervisor's job starting at 5:30 a.m. I took it in a minute. I'm glad I did because within another two weeks, the afternoon job opened and I moved right into that one. For me, that was great. At least, I worked every day and I supervised others. I've always been comfortable in a leadership position and I never really liked working for other people. In this job, I became the "go-to" guy for all supplies. I had cleaning supplies, trash bags, note paper, brushes, etc., anything you needed. As I said before, I had previously owned several businesses besides working with my father in our family business. But during those years, I never worked on my character because I was so caught up with the distractions. And, there were plenty of distractions! I lived in the past and held on to my nasty ways. But this time was different, because this time I recognized that I was actually different. I was a dry drug addict and alcoholic who *wanted* to live for the right reasons. The transformation had begun without fanfare, without notice.

In the ASAT program you meet so many different kinds of people with a variety of personalities, character traits, religious beliefs, etc. There are those who really want to change and there are those who just play the system and keep coming back through the system. There are those who have all the answers but never implement them. The "No Action Jacksons" who have great intentions but who never follow through. It really depends on the individual and how they digest the information, how they process what they learn. Thomas Henderson was so right when he said, "It's at the end of the day--after the program's done, that your day really begins. That's when you're left with no one to fool but yourself." I decided I would first learn how to be real with myself, and then I'd be real with others.

My time in ASAT was a true education. I looked forward to the group interaction and I really looked forward to searching for "Michael." I was like the lost treasure chest and the pieces of the treasure map were spread out among these people. Little by little I began putting the pieces of the puzzle together. There were many obstacles I had to climb over or just plow through. Sometimes we, ourselves, make it a harder challenge than it needs to be. Life is worth living and we should stop cheating ourselves out of a good life and start treating ourselves to a life filled with love and happiness. I'm here to tell you that you *don't* have to come to prison in order to wake up and smell the coffee. You just have to commit to the idea of having a good life and take steps, even small steps in the right direction. I know that sounds very simple. Drug addiction is a hard thing to overcome, but you know, it really is one step at a time. We are the ones that make taking the first step monumental.

I never tried the "fake-it-to-make it" theory. I couldn't understand why anyone would spend their time with no real accomplishment except for putting in a certain number of days for a completion of a course. I didn't want just a completion; I wanted the benefits of the knowledge I was supposed to gain. This was my *life* and it was time for me to learn all I could so that I would be able to fulfill my life's purpose. I now know that God has a bigger plan for me and it doesn't include being in prison.

Every day I took advantage of the program. I opened my eyes and I closed my mouth and that is a hard thing for me to do. I was determined to pay attention—again, a really hard thing for me to do.

The very best thing about the ASAT program was the help and support of the staff. We had daily contact with a team of dedicated counselors. I asked them question after question because they had unlimited access to the information I needed to make this transition. I couldn't get enough information. In program we discussed all kinds of things that revolved around our behavior. How was our behavior influenced by the world in which we lived? What part of our lives might have contributed to our eventual incarceration? Being able to identify these things was so important for recovery. Knowing the answers doesn't fix anything, but it puts it all into perspective.

To say Ms. D was my prison guardian angel doesn't come close. Her guidance and influence played an enormous part in my success. Once I started the program, I found out that there was an opportunity for an early release through the "Limited Time Credit Allowance Law (LTCA)." If I could qualify, I could earn up to six months "good time" which means less time to serve. Ms. D. got me into the first Inmate Program Aide (IPA) Training program at Mid-State Correctional under the LTCA Law. It was a two -year program that rewards you with a chance for a six-month early release. But, nothing was guaranteed. I have to admit that I felt privileged to be accepted into it but I understood that I might not actually be granted the six month early leave. You had to stay out of trouble, have two years of successful participation in a college program or you have to maintain a two-year IPA job.

There were only certain types of jobs that were classified as IPA jobs under this law like program aides or program facilitators, etc. Out of 1800 inmates I was one of 12 to make the list and, if you can believe it, at this time, I was the only one that didn't have an IPA job, which was a requirement. My paint crew job ended and there weren't any available jobs that qualified for IPA status. We all had to take the three-week training course to prepare us for the IPA positions. So every day, for the entire three weeks of training, I would remind Ms. D. and my teacher, Ms. V. that I had to find a job.

I've never been able to watch or wait for things to happen. Impatience is my middle name. To make matters worse, my Dad had this saying, "We're Tandois, we don't sit around and wait for things to happen, we make things happen." What that means to me is I can't jeopardize my life by placing my future in someone else's hands. I have to take control of my destiny; I have to steer my own ship. I have always taken that saying to heart. So, when Ms. D. said, "Don't worry, Tandoi, something will pop-up," I wasn't exactly comforted.

When I was 15-years-old, I needed a job. I decided I wanted to work in a bakery. My Dad was friends with a family who owned one, but they just weren't hiring at the time. So, I would call every day, sometimes twice a day. "Hi, this is Mike Tandoi, just checking to see if you need me to work today." Finally, after two weeks of constantly calling, I got hired. I made sure I was always on time and ready to work. I may have been the youngest kid on the job but I worked as hard as I could. They were never sorry that they hired me.

It was the same way in prison. I made a promise to myself that by time the three week training was over, I would have an IPA job and I was going to be part of this program no matter what! I knew this was a-once-in-a-lifetime opportunity and I wanted the opportunity even though there were no guarantees. I was willing to take the chance for the early release. I woke up every morning and thanked God for the chance. I prayed constantly asking Him to send me an IPA job.

I began the IPA training with a new-found energy and unbelievable hope! I loved this training. We would role play different types of scenarios which taught us how to get the attention of other inmates. We learned the dos and don'ts of the prison system. During the role playing, two or three guys would go through a skit that would place us in different situations dealing with prison life. I learned so much from these exercises.

Well, the day before my three-week training was finished I finally got a job offer…or I should say "offers." Life is never easy or simple. Ms. D. sat me down and said "I've found two job possibilities for you. I will let you choose." The first was working for Transitional Services and the supervisor had requested me. The other job was a Chapel Aide.

If you remember, when my father died, I was really mad at God. I completely stopped going to Church. I didn't want to hear the word "God." The Chapel Aide job was offered by Father Weber, the Catholic chaplain. After my father died and through most of my prison time, Father Weber had become a surrogate father to me. When Ms. D. spoke to Father about the job he said to her, "Tell Michael it is time to come home… he's taken enough time off."

So, from no job to two jobs, which one would I pick? I told Ms. D. that I wanted to work for the Church. "Send me home, Ms. D., send me home." Finally, I had a job that would count towards my possible early release.

From December 28, 2009 to February 22, 2010, I worked part time in the Chapel as an IPA clerk. I graduated from the ASAT program in February. Then, Ms. D. said she needed me to move into the MICA Dorm and she would hire me as an IPA for the dorm. An IPA for the dorm is something like a residence advisor (RA) in a college dorm. Ha, some college! It took me a couple of weeks before I was able to give her an answer. I was really hesitant to move into this dorm but my two friends, Nicky and Shawn, lived there. But, I was still unsure. You see, MICA stands for Mentally Ill Chemically Addicted. The 4-A MICA dorm had a bad reputation around the compound because everyone thought the dorm was filled with a bunch of crazies. In fact, it was referred to as the "Crazy House." Truthfully, some of the inmates were crazy and that name actually was a fairly accurate description of the place. It took me about two weeks, but, finally I agreed to move into the dorm as the IPA. I was hired to continue my recovery by helping others in need, the most needy of guys in the world. Again, from no job to two IPA jobs which exceeded the required status for the six month release program. Can you say, "Thank you, God"?

The first night I moved in I had to stay in a room with 11 other inmates. I was in 4-Bottom and I had a guy on the top bunk whose nickname was "Jackie Chan." Yes, just like in the movies. It wasn't until 3 a.m. my first night that I found out why he was called "Jackie Chan." "Jackie" woke up, jumped off his top bunk and landed on the top of his locker screaming and throwing Karate kicks and chops looking right at me. I jumped up out of a dead sleep and freaked out. "Jackie" just kept throwing his kicks and chops. To my amazement, this sort of thing happens all the time in 4A.

The next day I was moved to a four-man room which I thought was the best thing in the whole world except for one problem. I was in such a hurry to move that when Nicky and I moved my locker, we scratched the floor. Neither one of us realized it until later that day when I came back from my Chapel job to find my whole bedroom had been tossed. The C.O. flipped my locker, gave me a shake down and confiscated everything. She took my light, fan, radio, and even the carpet for my feet…everything!

Why was that? Because I damaged the floor! Well, I definitely marked it. The scratch must have been 25-feet long and she thought I did it on purpose. So now I was on the very top of her "hit-list." That was very bad because she could stir-up the pot really good so you'd get burned big time. Within a very short time, I learned that it was Ms. N's way or the highway. If she wanted you off the unit, you could be sure you would be off the unit. When I asked her where all my things were she flipped out! I knew I had to do something to fix this. When I actually went to look at the scratch I discovered that it really wasn't scratched, it was the rubber marking from one of the wheels on the cart we used to move my very overweight locker. So I spent the next few hours waxing and buffing the floor until it shined.

Fortunately, I am no longer on her hit list but that first couple of weeks she made my life miserable. When I finally ran into Mrs. D., I asked her, "What did you do to me? Last week my life was fine, now I'm living in the craziest house on the compound: Jackie Chan's jumping off lockers; I saw one of the inmates beat the crap out of another inmate just for some "recreation"; the C.O. wants me dead and I am sure I'm going to box any minute. What did you get me into?" Do you know what she said to me? Very calmly she said, "Don't worry, Tandoi, everything is going to be fine."

Believe it or not, I discovered that Mrs. N. was the best C.O. on the compound. She was one tough chick and she came to work each day ready for war and was always ready for the worse. Without her here, this place would have truly been an insane asylum.

Over two and a half years later I was still in 4-A. It had been a rocky road at times but it has been one of the very best things to come into my life, an actual blessing. I do admit, however, it took me a while to recognize the "blessing." My first year was a constant battle for respect. No one could figure out why I was there. Was I doing it because I had a good heart or was it because I was up to something?

I remember one particular day, I had just returned to the unit after I had finished giving a seminar on recovery. Eight of us from the house got thrown up against the wall because "someone" said we were all selling drugs. That was a lie, but standard procedure. The C.O.s flipped all of our lockers and dumped all of our belongings. The place looked like a dump yard. Of course, nothing was found so none of us could be moved off the unit. But that is just how chaotic things are in prison, all the time.

When I took the job at 4-A as the IPA, I didn't know what I was really getting myself into. What Ms. D. didn't tell me was that I had to "create" my own job description or else just go crazy along with the inmates. Many of the program aides just drift around not doing very much until they are told to do something. That just wasn't me. I treated this job as a brand new venture. I went in with my heart and soul. I delivered every single day for over two years. I would sit with my group five days a week and listen to everything my counselors said. When I said I grew to know that the move to MICA was a blessing, part of the reason was because of the counselors I had in the IPA training program. I had the Dream Team of Counselors, each of whom brought a different point of view on the world of recovery. They each worked tirelessly to deliver hope, inspiration and education in a place that is short on all of those things. I asked a thousand questions on all kinds of topics and there was always one of them who had the answer for me.

Part of my job was to facilitate group discussions with my dorm mates. I wrote up presentations and seminars based on the life issues all inmates face. Issues like family problems, relationships, how to deal with being away from home and how to overcome addiction. I am so proud of the level of motivation I was able to instill into my fellow inmates. In the program I would meet guys who had been through the program three or four times. ASAT is really designed as a one-time program. So I would ask the returning guys questions like, "What did you forget to do, or what did you leave behind that was so important that you had to come back"? I would just sit back to see how they acted in the group. It was so clear to me that they didn't want what the program offered. They thought that just being physically present in a program was enough. It's not. You have to make the program part of you. Life is worth living, but you have to ask, "What can I bring to the party"?

The problems inmates face aren't really so different from those on the outside except for one thing. We are all criminals. Innately we shouldn't be trusted. That may sound strange to you, but it is true. If you don't have anyone around you that you feel you can trust, you certainly don't let your guard down. I'd have to say the biggest problem we have is loneliness. You can be in a dorm with 50 people, but you still feel all alone.

I remember the day when we were in program and I realized that "Cheech" wasn't in the room, as he should have been. One of the guys and I went to see if he was in his room. As we walked into the room, "Cheech" jumped from the top of his locker in an effort to commit suicide. He had tied his bed sheet around the fire sprinkler pole so he could hang himself. If we hadn't come in right at that moment he would have killed himself. Why? He was missing his family so much and all he wanted was to hear his mother's voice on the phone. All he needed that day was a simple phone call. However, he had burned so many bridges so many times that his family was trying some tough love which now included complete isolation from him.

A simple piece of mail means the world to us. Every day at 3:30 p.m.

the mail list goes up and everyone in the system makes sure that they check the list to see if they have mail. Years go by for some and no mail ever shows up. Their name is never on the list.

There was one guy who actually told me that he hated me every day for 15 minutes. It starts at about 3:30 because I receive mail and I cook my own meals. He envies that. This guy has been down for a very serious crime and was sentenced 15 years to life. He has been serving time since 1987. Most of his family has either passed away or are just too busy with their lives to think about him anymore. This is only one example but these are the guys that taught me about simple compassion—yes, even for a criminal, compassion is so important. A simple "Hello", or a little bit of recognition means so much. Guys with families have to live with the reality that they have no control in the lives of their wives, children, or even their parents. When kids get in trouble or someone gets sick or worse, a family member dies, it is excruciating to know that there isn't one thing you can do to help. Just today, one of the guys looked really down in the dumps and I asked him what was wrong? He said, "Tandoi, you really want to know"? I said, "Of course, I want to know." He replied, "I woke up today."

In every one of my seminars, I stress the importance of family. Even if you never respected or appreciated family before, you can start now. When you get back home, it will be hard enough to win their trust but it is all worth the fight. When kids come up to visit their fathers and it's time for them to leave, you have no idea how much your heart breaks when you hear, "No, daddy, please don't go." No matter how much of a hardened criminal you might have been, the sound of those voices breaks your heart into a million pieces. That's the part that gets to me every time I am on a visit and I see these little kids. I don't know what I would do if those children were mine.

I have a niece who was just a little girl when I came to prison. I've written her letters the entire time I have been incarcerated. Her mother wrote to me twice when I first got sent up. I have written at least one letter every month for all these years. I've sent birthday cards, Christmas cards and pictures of Uncle Mike. But after those first two letters, I have never received another. I honestly tired to keep some kind of a relationship with my niece. I don't know if her mom ever told her how much Uncle Mike loves her. It hurts me a lot. But I remember at the beginning of my bid, there was a guy who said, "No matter what, always write your family. Even if they never write back, don't ever stop writing." So, I keep writing.

One of my favorite seminars was called "Sick." I talked about how we all came into prison sick. We were sick from drugs or alcohol abuse or from the crimes we committed. We go through the system and we do our time. We don't make any changes to overcome our sickness. We leave prison and, because we left as sick as when we first came, we return even sicker than before. The question is how can we stop this from happening again and again? How is recovery possible? This presentation was really well received and judging from the comments from the inmates, I think some took it to heart. That made me feel all the more determined to continue to find ways to reach these guys. It was then that I made an amazing discovery. By reaching the guys I was reaching me, too.

But, there were countless times that I was disappointed when someone I was working with got into trouble and ended up in the box or shipped off to another dorm. I worked hard trying to give the guys hope for a new future. I wanted so much for them to believe that it was possible to dig out of the mess we put ourselves in. That was my whole goal and I began to know that I wanted to give back because I now realized how thankful I was that God had given me a second chance to "do it right."

The transition into the MICA dorm was hard. Besides the problem with the C.O., I also had to overcome the petty jealousy and immaturity of the inmates around me. Let's just say that none of us were stellar individuals. That's easy to say now, but let me tell you, some crazy things happened. Like when "snitch notes" get dropped. Yes, I said "snitch" just like in grammar school.

Writing a snitch note is a way for an inmate to anonymously "tell" on another inmate. One day, Ms. D. came to me and asked," Mr. Tandoi, are you eating your dinner on the porch with Nicky"? I replied, "Well, yes I am. I cook every night around the time the guys go to the mess hall. Why do you ask"? She said, "I want you to think about how it must look when you are eating the five-course meals that you cook in front of a bunch of guys who don't have as much as you." I said, "Truthfully, Ms. D. a lot of these guys burned their bridges. I was smart enough not to burn my bridges and so I'm able to afford to cook my own meals. Besides, cooking is the only thing that I truly enjoy doing. I take pride in my cooking." Then she said, "I understand that, Mr. Tandoi, but can you just eat in your room from now on"? "Ms. D., are you telling me that someone actually "told" on me for eating my dinner"? That's a new level of snitch note. I've never heard of anyone ever getting a snitch note for cooking and eating. But, that is how it goes down in prison.

I've always loved to eat but now I discovered that I loved to cook, too, even though my appliances consisted of a microwave, toaster oven and hot pot. In my family, meals were very important. I've already told you that we always ate together. No matter what happened, at the end of the day we sat down together and shared the meal. So, the idea of a "meal time" was second nature to me. I just had to figure out a way to get these guys from telling on me for eating. This snitch note incident happened right before Thanksgiving. So, I asked the guys if they wanted to throw a Thanksgiving Dinner. Everyone was invited. If you're going to get to a man's heart you have to go through his stomach first. So we planned a real Thanksgiving Day Dinner almost like the ones we had at home. We had turkey, ham, potatoes, and for dessert—cheesecake. You have never had cheesecake like I make in the microwave. After that, there were no more snitch notes. Not only had I won them over, but it was the first time that we worked together to accomplish a common goal. At the end of the meal, one of the inmates came up to me and said, "Thanks, Tandoi, this is the nicest thing anyone ever did for me."

Yes, I had won over the guys, but trouble was lurking around the corner. For the next several years we continued to throw the Thanksgiving Day dinner. From the first year to the present, each year the dinner got bigger. Instead of me providing most of the food, which was pretty hard for me to do, I involved all the inmates from our dorm—46 to be exact.

We would sit down and decide the menu, and then I'd figure out how much it would cost each participant. I made out the shopping list and then everyone had to follow through and buy their assigned items at the Commissary Store. It turned out that we could make the dinner happen if each participant contributed $5.00 of his bi-weekly purchase from the store. Now, $5.00 doesn't sound like anything except for the fact that most inmates earn $4.30 every two weeks. So, $5.00 is a fortune! Also some inmates smoked so they had to take cigarette money out of their earnings, too. But, all the effort and work paid off. This dinner brought a ray of light to a place that breeds mostly darkness. It brought a sense of normalcy where nothing is normal. It really is something to see this group of men who come from all walks of life, who have committed just about every crime known to man sit down and enjoy a holiday meal together. Some of the guys actually came up to me to say that they had never had a Thanksgiving Dinner. Talk about the haves and those who have not.

You can't have Thanksgiving without a turkey, right? Actually getting the turkey was the trickiest part. Each year my mother and grandmother donated three turkeys—real turkeys, not processed turkey. I would have to give up my monthly 35-pound food package allotment because the turkeys took the place of my monthly "care package." I had no idea how important this event would become to everyone. It was as close as we could get to being home with family for a holiday.

I would get permission from the prison and everything went great, well, that is until this past year. My Mom bought the turkeys and made plans to visit me so that she could bring me the turkeys. Even my step dad had to get involved because I couldn't receive all three turkeys at once because the total weight was over 35 pounds. So, my step dad had to "visit" another inmate so that he could drop off one of the turkeys to someone else other than me.

Everything went fine except for the fact that when my Mom and Stepdad left, the corrections officer gave them back the turkeys. He told my Mom that they were not allowed. She said that she had done this for many years and it was always allowed before. The office explained that they were no longer allowed because of the" bones." (I guess it would be possible for an inmate to make a weapon from the turkey bones, but it hadn't ever happened before.) So my Mom asked if she could please see a Sergeant. To make a long story short, my Mom tells the Sergeant about the problem. He knows me and knows that we have done this dinner each year so he approved the turkeys. But that is only the beginning of this problem. It gets worse. You see, the turkeys were denied by one sergeant and now a different sergeant approved the package. In prison terms, this is very bad. But since the sergeant approved the turkeys, my friend and I brought them back to the dorm to put them in the ready-made ice boxes we had waiting. Everyone is crazy with excitement because we have three *real* turkeys.

The next day, I went down to make plans to pick up the paper supplies we needed. The Church donates all the paper and utensil supplies and the Recreation Department lets us use the coffee maker along with enough coffee for 200 cups, sugar and creamer plus Kool-Aid. So, as you can see, this is an enormous undertaking and really is a "community project."

You might wonder why we worked so hard at all of this. Well, this is a therapeutic community. We are supposed to experience things like this especially when we want inmates to realize that recovery is possible. This is what can happen when we are clean and sober.

The day before the big event, I got called out of my job. The correction officer said, "Tandoi, the Package Room Sergeant wants to see you in Building 101." I had a bad feeling about this. I just felt something really bad was about to happen.

I rushed over to the building to see what this was all about. The Sergeant approached me in the hall and started to talk to me about the turkeys. Now, this is the same officer that denied the turkey package. He told me to sit at a table and said, "I'm going to be honest with you, Tandoi, not me but another sergeant (this is a big lie), feels like he got played over these turkeys." I'm thinking this is not making any sense. Then he said, "But I can tell you that there are two options. Option #1, you can get the turkeys and turn them over to me— you still have them, right? Option #2 is you can go to the box. Either way, I can tell you that you are not going to eat those turkeys."

"Well, Sergeant, I guess you made up my mind for me, I'm giving you the turkeys." Then he said, "I'll tell you what, I know about three turkeys but I'm only looking for two." Now, here is where I would have normally said, "Really, just two"? But, after all these years in prison, I've learned how some of these guys work. You see, I would have given him two turkeys and then he would have come back to the dorm to find the other turkey and I would have been in the box anyway. But at this point, I was dumbfounded.

I went back to the dorm and, fortunately, I ran into Ms. D. on the walkway. I was in a deep panic and told her what had just happened. She asked me to wait so that she could make a few calls. I said, "Ms. D. please, no favors. My Dad just spoke to me from Heaven and he said, "Let them have the turkeys. We've taken bigger hits than this, kid." This is the point where I asked to go the Church. In prison, the Church is considered a "safe place." I've always run to the Church when I was in I trouble, why not now? I had to get "home." Once I got to Church, I broke down and I cried. A grown man cried over turkeys. I was overwhelmed by the fact that I would have to tell my mother that the turkeys got high-jacked. Then, I would have to tell the guys that we weren't going to have turkey for Thanksgiving Dinner. I just didn't know how I would tell them.

Father Weber, Reverend Elis and two counselors met to discuss this situation. Everyone was shocked at what happened over some turkeys.

Now, remember, we are in prison. When someone steals a can of coffee it is usually because there are drugs in the can--but turkeys? In the end, we pulled a fast one and donated all three of the turkeys to a mission in town. We didn't have turkey for dinner but we still had our meal together. I gave thanks because I didn't go to the box, but it was very close. I was doing the right thing and trouble still found me. That's how it happens in prison—what's up is down and what's down is up!

Actually, one of the hardest things for me to adjust to in prison was the food. At Groveland and at Mid-State, each dorm had its own kitchen. The kitchen was located in the "community day room" which is also used for classes, meetings, watching TV, etc. This room is shared by everyone. The kitchen is not the shiny, fully stocked kitchen like home, but it's a kitchen that we are allowed use to cook our own meals. The appliances consisted of a microwave and a toaster oven, hot pot and ice machine. If something breaks, we have to put in a work order and hope for the best. Remember, things in prison either take really long or happen really fast. The utensils consisted of plastic knives and forks and spoons. There are very few spices available: adobo, oregano and garlic, and curry. There is only one word that describes my microwave meals and that word is "magical." I can turn something small into the biggest, most unbelievably fabulous tasting food you have ever had. In fact, the phrase, "Tandoi dishes are Tando-licious" was born at Mid-State.

If you're going to do time, chances are you're doing it broke! I have been fortunate, because for the most part, I have had a job while in prison. Inmates earn from between 10 cents to 26 cents an hour depending on the job. Not everyone has a "job." Even if you do, it is really hard to earn enough money to support your food allowance of $27.50/wk. You have to depend on family or friends to send you money so you can buy your food supplies. They don't usually send you very much money at one time. If you don't budget your money and keep a balance in your account, by the time any additional money actually reaches you, your account is depleted and it's a day too late to go shopping. If that happens, you have to wait another two weeks before you can go shopping again. The first thing I mastered was how to plan for two weeks of food. I learned that in a community, if you pool your resources everybody's money goes a lot farther. So, in my dorm, most of us contribute to the meals and we shop according to what we are going to eat for the next two weeks. If you don't contribute, you don't eat with the community. Some of the guys eat all their meals in the dorm; some guys only eat a couple of meals a week with us. If you don't eat here, you can eat in the Mess Hall where you don't use any money from your account.

I've already told you the grocery store is the Commissary Store and it was one of my favorite places in the whole prison. Inmates are allowed to spend $55 for a two-week food allotment. If you cook three meals a day for two weeks, $55 cuts it really close unless you are creative. Having the ability to cook my own meals is how I fell in love with cooking. I am the king of the microwave meal and it was one of the positive things I learned from my stay here. It was trial and error all the way and I definitely messed up some meals. One time I was cooking a sauce meal with one of my Italian friends, Mike. He noticed that I put some jalapeño peppers in the sauce and he didn't like jalapeño peppers. So, he dumped the whole bottle of jalapeños into the sauce. The worst sauce I've ever made! Another time, I overcooked some Cactus Annie taco shells and my boy, Jackson, took it upon himself to throw the tacos all over the wall! Another mess!

But nothing tops the Nicky "Thumbs" experience. First of all, Nicky was the best kid I ever met. I say "kid" because he was only 17 years old when he came to prison. We trusted each other from the very beginning. One time on a visit, his mother pulled me aside and said, "Michael, I trust that you will never let anything bad happen to my son." That was it, our fate was sealed. No matter how tough the times were we were always there for each other. Nicky became my brother from another mother.

One Friday night I was cooking a red sauce loaded with meat, Italian sausage, meat balls, pepperoni, and summer sausage. This sauce was out of this world. I sent Nicky to rinse off the two pounds of ziti macaroni when I noticed he had been gone for 10 minutes. So I went to check on him and the sight I saw was priceless. Nicky was scooping up macaroni from off the floor using his ID card because he had spilled the macaroni. Mind you, this is a community slop sink area where people do all kinds of things. You name it, and it goes in this sink. If I hadn't found him, we would have eaten ziti from off the floor. I flipped out, because I thought he would poison us and I made him throw all the macaroni away and we cooked another two pounds of ziti.

My Dad loved to cook, too. He made the best stuffed pizza in the world. It was an unwritten rule that he always made the pizzas for Christmas Eve. Christmas Eve was at my Aunt Bonnie's house, my Dad's older sister. Then when my cousin Joelle (Aunt Bonnie's daughter) got married, the feast moved to Joelle's house. It was the typical Italian Christmas Eve. We had stuffed calamari, shrimp, beef cutlets, olive salad, fried rappi and my Dad always brought the stuffed pizza—two huge crescent-shaped pizzas. One pizza was sausage, peppers and hot pepper cheese and the other was a stuffed olive and scallion pizza. Oh my God! It was heaven on earth. But the very best part was the tradition of just being with family! When I get home, stuffed pizza will be one of the first things I make. I'm going to fill in for my Dad. That is one way he will always be with us.

As I started to say, I was now in the early release program, I have a qualifying job and there was one last item that still needed to be attended to. To ensure my chances for early release, I had to be in a two-year college program. In March of 2010 I enrolled in the Small Business Management Program at Penn Foster Career College. This was one of only a very few colleges that offered courses totally through correspondence—not electronically. In prison, you have no access to the Internet so I could not take amy courses via On-Line Learning.

My Aunt Bonnie realized that if I stood any chance in life, I needed some kind of formal education. As it is, when I get out of prison, I will always have a felony on my record, so a little bit of college might help me overcome some part of that stigma. Aunt Bonnie and I have always had a special relationship. When I was little and I had to do a project for school, I got shipped over to her house so that I could get it done. She was the one who, when I graduated from high school, just about got on her knees to beg me to take just one college course. She always recognized that I had an aptitude for business and she felt that it would be good for me to learn how to run a business in a proper and business-like manner. Of course, I was much too busy with my life adventures to even consider that. Besides, I never had success in school and the last thing I wanted to do was more school work.

In one of her letters to me, Aunt Bonnie said, "Michael, wouldn't this be a good time to take a college course? You don't have any outside distractions and you have the time to devote to it. I found a college that offers correspondence courses. Let me send you the information and see what you think? If you see anything you would like to take, I will pay for the course. All you have to do is promise to do the best you can." Just like when I was a kid, she guided me through this "project" too. Out of the blue she provided the chance to complete the early release program. She put the tools in my hands. All I had to do was to pick them up and use them.

The Small Business Management course looked like something I would be interested in taking. And so I started. Ironically, I didn't find it hard at all. Some of the information was challenging to understand, but I got through it. I found out that I actually got excited by the things I learned. The final course project was to develop an actual business plan for a prospective company. My college experience was great. I was able to learn so much about business from a legal and financial aspect. I've owned businesses before, but I found out that I never ran them correctly. Why, because I didn't know how! Whatever I did, I did by the seat of my pants. Whatever problem came up, I solved it but I never looked at the business as a whole nor did I plan for the future. I had a million great ideas, but not one plan.

I would call my aunt every Sunday night and we would talk about the course. She actually works at a college in Rochester and she was able to get me an outline of a sample business plan from a faculty member she knew. I had no idea what it should even look like. I would hand write my answers to each part of the outline, and send it to her in the mail. She would then type it up for me. She would read it over and say, "Michael, this needs to be expanded, or you know what you are missing here is… Then from my textbooks and limited prison resources, I would make the correction or addition and send them back to her.

Almost every week, I would call her and say, Aunt Bon, I think I want to do my business plan on this type of business. The next week it would be a different business. This went on for weeks. And, just like she did when I was 12 years old and we were putting together a school project, she said, "Michael, focus! Write your plan on something you know. This isn't your life's work; it is just a school project." Her words finally sunk in and I chose to write my business plan on the development of an asphalt company. You have to remember, I had no access to Internet so I had to do my "research" from what I knew. My Dad ran his asphalt company for 32 years and I was right by his side so I did know about this type of company. When I needed demographics, she would research it for me. Then she would send it all to me and I would decide what to include in the plan. To supplement my research, she gave me a subscription to "Fortune 500 Magazine." The last part of this "project" was the financial section. I knew the numbers, but I didn't know how to put them into a spread sheet. So, Tammy, my Dad's former secretary, the same Tammy who got me to Conesus Lake after the shooting, saved the day again. She took all my numbers and put them on the spreadsheet. So, as you can see, it really does "take a village."

When it was time for me to get the grade for the business plan, I was really nervous. My aunt kept telling me, "Michael, I don't want you to be disappointed. Your business plan is terrific but, remember, there are pieces you just cannot submit. I don't know how much that might reduce your score. Let's write a letter to the instructor and put it in the front of the plan just to acknowledge that you realize there are a few required items that you cannot provide, like applying for a bank loan." So I wrote the letter and submitted the business plan. It was the most beautiful thing I ever saw—a real work of art, if I say so myself. I was so proud of the job I had done. It took almost five months to put together, but it was so worth it.

Getting my grades was another thing we overcame. You see, they were posted on line, and there was no way for me to get them. Aunt Bon got permission from the college so that she could get them for me. Again, on Sunday, I would ask, "Are my grades posted"? When I was in high school, if I somehow managed to get a C in a course, I thought I did great. But now when each chapter test turned out to be an A, I was shocked and ecstatic and I wanted more A's. Sometimes, the grades didn't get posted as fast as I thought they should especially when I found the chapter to be a harder chapter to learn. On those chapters, she would send me the grade printout through the mail so I didn't have to wait until the next Sunday. On the printout, she would make a huge explanation point and say, "Wow, thought this was a hard chapter. Too bad you only got an A." I was never so excited to see my grades and to learn that I finished the course with an A—one of the very few of my entire school experience except, of course, for gym. By the way, I got 100% on my business plan. I was always too cool to worry about my grades. But, now I understood the feeling of pride and satisfaction in getting good grades. All I can say is its amazing.

So for the next two years I maintained the IPA job and continued with my college work because my ultimate goal was to get that six month early release date. To me, that was huge. One less Christmas, one less New Year's, one less Thanksgiving, one less birthday I would have to spend away from my family. I was willing to climb any mountain to get back home to them.

Ah, but like I've said before, in prison, things change and they change fast! From December 28, 2009 to May 5, 2010, I was the Chapel Aide IPA and I thought everything was going along great, maybe too great. The State decided to change the job title to Administrative Clerk. That meant that the job no longer held an IPA status. The worst part was the fact that we were never notified of the change. I found out totally by accident.

Nicky asked Ms. D. to run his dates. He wanted to figure out when he would qualify for his IPA. He also worked in the Chapel with me. When she noticed the change in his title, she ran my dates, too, and saw that my job title had also changed! The reason for the change was the State no longer felt the Chapel Aide position met the qualifications for IPA status. Can you say, "Oh, my God?" I wasn't too affected because my MICA job also had IPA status, but Nicky got burned for four months and he had to catch up. I stayed in the Chapel position even though the status changed. I needed to be there with or without the IPA credit. The Church had become the foundation of who I was. My blessings continued each morning when I entered the Church and splashed holy water on my face.

It's true, I took the IPA work because of the early release but then I fell in love with the work I was doing. Because of my job in the Prison Chapel, each morning I would tell the guys on the MICA unit that I was leaving for work so that I could go pray for them because we all needed prayer.

I have come to recognize and accept the fact that, without God in my life, none of this would have been possible. The average length of service for a clerk on the MICA unit is two months. That is because the IPAs start losing their minds and they run from the program. Patience was one of the things I had to master in order for me to grow. I have learned to be patient with others and compassionate with the inmate population.

The MICA unit was the most talked about dorm throughout the compound because everyone thought we were a brunch of crazies and me being the craziest! Strange as it may seem, being in the MICA unit turned out to be my ultimate blessing from God. I have been able to give back and help others who are completely lost. I know what "lost" is. Many of these guys have little or no means of finding their way on the road to recovery by themselves. Helping them to find their way has been magical for me. It keeps me full of the Spirit and that makes me want to do more.

CHAPTER 5

Recovery

THE FIRST TIME I ENTERED the Chapel of St. Dismas as a Chapel Aide, I could feel that this job, in this place, was entirely different from any other job I have ever had. I was known as the facility "bad boy." Everyone, especially Father Weber took a big chance on me. The Chapel job is probably the hardest job to get at Mid-State. You can't just apply for the position. This was one of those jobs where the Priest hand-selects the aide. I was just really lucky, because Father actually didn't select me. It was Ms. D. who dropped me off at his doorstep, similar to an abandoned baby being left on the church steps. But in the end, it was Father who sent word to Ms. D. to, "Tell Michael, it's time to come home." I had never considered a church, let alone a prison church, as being a home. But that is exactly what it came to be. Throughout my years of addiction, churches were the only place that I ever found safety from my demons. If I had been allowed to sleep in St. Dismas Chapel, I would have.

I was introduced to two other Chapel Aides during the first week on the job. One still remains and the other left five months after I started. My task that first week was to set up three Christmas trees, complete with lights and ornaments. I pretended that I had just gone to cut down the trees with my imaginary children, we then loaded them into my truck and brought them back to our imaginary house because the imaginary family was coming over for a tree-trimming party. It was so real to me and I found the experience so very comforting. Never in my wildest dreams could I have imagined that this feeling would come in a prison Church. I knew there were no children, no house and no party but the feeling was wonderful just the same.

From that very first step into the house of the Lord, I was so happy and felt so at peace. Remember I have been talking to God my whole life. I wasn't exactly spiritually dead, but whenever I would talk to God, it was because I was in trouble or I wanted something. This time was different. I didn't ask for anything—I just wanted to give. It was so good to not have to live up to the "bad boy" image I had.

So I started at the bottom. I had to work my way up slowly. It took a while to get rid of that bad boy tag that was actually a yoke around my neck. I would listen to the Chaplains, Father Weber, Reverend Ellis and Imam Montiero, when they spoke. I would hear the Reverend say things like," God didn't send Jesus for the healthy, he sent Jesus for the sick; He didn't send Him for the good but for the really bad." After a time I found that the Reverend and I had quite a bit in common and we eventually became Bible buddies.

But before that time came, I was cleaning the Church toilets, mopping floors and doing the dirty work. I would leave the Church and go back to the compound and live a double life because I thought they were two different worlds. The Church being one world and the prison compound another. I'm not sure why I thought that but I guess I didn't know that I should be able to move from one to the other seamlessly. I didn't understand that real change is for every minute of the day not just for certain times or places. It could have been that I was still under the spell that clouded my understanding of what real change was and how it had to go right down to your very soul in order for it to cause permanent change. Whatever the reasons were I lived a double life. It was like living with one girl and cheating on her with another girl. I would be at Church from 8 a.m. to 11 a.m., Monday to Friday, and Saturday night Mass from 6 to 8 p.m. then right back to the old ways. When my shift was over, I would go back to the compound and pick up where I left off. I would run around the facility, talk with a reckless mouth, buy and sell porn magazines. I didn't internalize what I was learning in the Chapel. I didn't allow myself to shed the old person I used to be. Maybe I was still scared or maybe I still didn't think it was possible to change. At first, I didn't even notice that I was changing, but very slowly, I did change.

The apostle Paul said, "And I was among the worse." Paul was one of those people who crucified those who proclaimed Jesus as the Savior. He actually killed Christians! God forgave him and called him into his service. So, why can't God change me? If Paul can change, then there must be hope for all of us bad boys—the black sheep of our families. I spent my first year in the Church going through the motions but with a wide open heart. Father Weber always called us his sheep. Every morning he would come to work and his sheep would be waiting for him at the door. I really started to feel a sense of family here. I began to feel like I belonged and that I actually was being accepted solely for who I was.

After the Christmas trees, my next responsibility was almost my last. I was in charge of taking care of the plants. Father walked me around one day and showed me all the plants and asked if I knew how to water plants. I said, "Of course, I do." So I watered the plants. But it turned out that I was watering the plants all wrong. Apparently, I wasn't giving them enough water. So one day, when I was in the afternoon ASAT program, the C.O. called out my name. "Tandoi, grab your stuff and come with me." Oh, no, what did I do now? He said, "You have to go down to the Chapel to see Father Weber." My heart sank. Oh God, who died now? That's the only reason anyone gets called down to Father's office during the day.

As I walked, I prayed, "Please, God, please don't let anyone in my family be dead." I got to Father's office and he sat me down and said, "You can take that look off your face, no one in your family is dead today, but your plants are!" "What, are you serious, Father?" He explained how important those plants were to him. I told him I understood and I did water them, but I guess not enough. So he gave me a lesson on how to water plants and since then I've fallen in love with every plant we have. I've lost a couple but I've learned how to tend to a plant. I talk to them, name them and, most importantly, I water them the right way. They say if you can keep a plant alive for a year, then you are ready to date. Well, I've kept these plants alive for way more than a year. Looks like I'm more than ready.

When my Dad died I kept asking God, "Why did you take my father from me? I need him more now than ever." I would yell out to God, "How could you do this to me?" You know, God answered me more than once when I cried out to him. "God answers those who cry out to him even in anger." I truly believe God has allowed my father's spirit to live in me. There are times I can actually feel my father. He may have called my Dad home, but He made sure I had Father Weber. I am so grateful to Father for taking a huge gamble on me. But he will cash out with a heavenly reward some day because I did complete the journey and I did grow to be a man because of Father's influence.

But, I can tell you it wasn't all holy water and rosary beads. There were plenty of times when Father yelled at me. He always called me out on my dirt. In case you don't know, the priest in a prison is just like the priest on the streets. He's the man with all the "juice." He finds out everything, so if I was doing dirt on the compound, he would sit me down and school me with his "pearls" from Heaven. And I listened. In fact, the truth was I listened to him more than I ever listened to any other person. That was because of a few reasons. First, there was no way to bribe him like I could with my Dad. Then, there is the fact that he didn't have to go out of his way to teach me right from wrong, but he did. He cared enough to make sure I learned.

During my first three years in prison, I was a porn freak! I owned and subscribed to every porn magazine in America. I was buying books in the yard every night. I had so much porn I had to send it home with friends when they came to visit me. I had to ask them to take it because I didn't have enough room to keep them all and they were so precious to me that I couldn't bear to throw them away. I was sick with these magazines. I actually studied them, memorizing each and every detail. Can you imagine what a scum bag I was? I actually cherished these magazines.

Father Weber had the job of media reviewer for all my porn books. Before I could get any publication, it had to get past Father first. He never asked me about them. He just waited patiently for me to open the door and one day I asked him if he thought it was wrong that I was obsessed with these books. Was it wrong for me to look at porn every night? After all, I was in prison what else was there to do?

That's all it took. I had opened the door that remained opened until I was able to filter out all the smut from my life. I would think to myself, priests don't ever have sex and Father seems extremely happy and at peace. I don't understand. I started to pray for the answer. And, God started working on me—slowly.

I will never forget my first major porn breakdown. It was a beautiful Saturday morning and I woke up at 8 a.m. My locker doors were wide open and they looked like the customary "porn doors." Every inch of my locker was covered with naked, hardcore porn. Each day the devil would work his black magic with those pictures. It was as though God would bless me and the devil would laugh and say, "Keep on blessing him, God, because I am going to continue to steal away that blessing." That morning I swear those girls were talking to me. "Come on Mike, lets party." If you have ever partied a lot, I don't care how hot the girls are, you reach a time when it's simply time to go! And that was exactly how I felt. "It's time for you to go. Get out of my life!" I started to tear down every inch of those doors. Nicky woke up and, at first, he just looked at me and thought, "Mike's lost his mind." Cheech tried to stop me because he wanted my shrine. I threw him off of me and continued to rip and smash everything. The doors came flying off. My porn magazines, 42 issues to be exact, were ripped to shreds. I ripped those books so much that I tore open my finger and left a cut that took several months to heal.

I filled two large garbage bags with torn magazines. But, you know, I felt great! I felt free. I could actually feel the Holy Spirit in my room for the first time. I wasn't in Church; I was in my own room and the Holy Spirit still found me. I had conquered the devil. I couldn't wait to see Father Weber so I could tell him what happened.

Well, that incident must have really made the devil mad and he wanted me back. I stayed strong for two weeks, and then, little by little, the monthly subscriptions starting arriving. I started looking at the magazines, and then I started to save one or two and it was a constant battle for the next two years. Father Weber, Reverend Ellis and Imam Montiero were there to guide me through the ordeal. Whenever I would feel like it was becoming a problem, I would run to the Church with a duffel bag filled with books and whoever was working that day got to be part of the madness. Once I brought 26 porn magazines to Church with me because I wanted to rip them up, but this time I wasn't going to use my hands. So Reverend Ellis and I went to the Law Library to use the paper shredder. But, we broke the shredder! It overheated and we actually ended up tearing them up by hand.

Today, I can honestly say that the burden of all of that has been lifted from me. Today, instead of smutty magazines, I have several Bibles to read. Now, the pictures in my room are of my family and friends. Both Father Weber and Reverend Ellis have been to my dorm room and they both are proud to see the great change. It wasn't a perfect, one-shot transition but whenever Father would get messages that I had slipped, he would always be there to catch me. I owe him so much.

It doesn't matter if you are addicted to drugs, cigarettes, alcohol, porn magazines, or whatever, you are still addicted. If you can overcome one addiction, you can overcome others. That is what I learned from that experience. I am now in control of my actions and through it all I found that I developed a respect for women that I hadn't had before.

If I hadn't had the example and help from Father Weber and Reverend Ellis, I'm not sure I would have succeeded as well with recovery. Father Weber was a surrogate father but Reverend Ellis was my cool uncle. I felt more comfortable talking to "Rev" about some things that I might not want to talk to Father about. I would ask him a million questions and enjoyed the time spent together. There was a time I didn't like Reverend Ellis, but it wasn't his fault, it was mine. I'm pretty sure he felt the same way about me, too. Those were my "punk" years when I didn't have time for anything that didn't benefit me or my next scam. But it was Reverend Ellis who got me home to see my Dad the day before he died. He could have very easily "blown me off" or dragged his feet. But he didn't. He got me home in record time and I will never forget that. Now, we have a great working relationship. We help each other with our sermons; we talk about God and His great works and about the real world. Most importantly, we ended up developing a respect for each other and it was the "Rev" who taught me how to pray out loud.

Imam Montiero was the head Muslim for our community. He prays five times a day, and he raises his family in the strict Muslim tradition. What I think makes him so unique is that he is my age. He is the most knowledgeable 32 year old I have ever met. Although we have many, many differences we never bash each other. Again, it's that respect level that I value so much. That's probably because in prison, there is so little respect for anything. Inmates certainly are not respected on any level because, well, we are inmates. There is so little personal dignity and I guess that is part of the "tearing down" process that needs to happen before anyone can really start to "recover." That was one of the hardest things I had to learn to accept.

The Imam was famous for asking me questions that he knew would create controversy. In his belief, he cannot understand why I would pray to Mother Mary and we discussed this topic a lot. I believe in my heart that Mother Mary is in Heaven keeping a close eye on me. After all, she is Jesus' mother. What son in his right mind would ignore his mother? I think she is a key to having my prayers answered. You may think this is very simplistic, but remember I was still searching for that child so that I could regain the kingdom of Heaven.

I have to say that I learned a great deal from the conversations I had with the Imam. He made me think. He made me verbalize my beliefs which helped clarify them in my own mind. I always looked forward to our talks and I will always value his friendship. The Imam was the person who called me in from cutting grass to tell me my father had passed. I will never forget his kindness to me that day. All three of these men were major contributors to my change from the old Michael to the one I am today. They are my personal Blessed Trinity.

As I said before, I had to work my way up as a Chapel Aide. The next task I was "trusted" with was cards. I became the card man. A big part of the Aide position dealt with secretarial work in the Office of the Chaplain. My main job in the morning was to handle the mail. I would get all the inmate mail that requested cards, Bibles or any type of spiritual literature for all of the religions.

A long time ago, Father Weber started the card program. In this program, inmates could write the Church to request up to three cards a month. These cards ranged from birthday to get wells cards all the way to I miss you and sympathy cards. We had them for every holiday and just about every kind of event. When Rob, the guy before me went home, I got "promoted" to this task. Actually the guy before Rob ended up in the "box" for six months because he high-jacked a whole case of cards and tried to sell them in the compound! He got caught and Father made sure he went down for it—six months is a long box time.

Now that I was the card guy, I would get harassed constantly. I'd be on the walkway or in the chow line and guys would scream out, "Yo, Tandoi, I need cards, Bro, send them." I would just say, "No problem, just send us a letter, tell me what you need and I'll send them right away."

That was the right way of getting cards and it was time we all learned about the "right way."

Sticking to the right way was so hard to do because inmates are the neediest people imaginable. Fighting off these requests without a formal request letter became a job all on its own. Once, I got a request through the facility mail that was addressed to Deacon Tandoi. Oh man, did I get in trouble for that! Both Father Weber and Reverend Elis weren't too happy with that, but the "Rev" said it wasn't my fault and that Deacon Tandoi actually sounded pretty good.

My Church job was never meant to be a job that I took for the paycheck. My experience with the Church was more of a "co-op" position. It was a learn-as-you-go process where I learned how to live a better life. When I walked in that first day, I thought I knew all there was to know. But in truth, I knew nothing. Then, ever so slowly, right before my eyes a new family emerged. Father Weber had the role of the father, the Reverend was my uncle and the Imam became the friend I never had on the street. They became role models for me especially when it came to family values. My life, like most of the guys here, was messed up—big time. The tearing down and rebuilding of Michael was a difficult process. I had to shed so many bad habits and corrupt ways of thinking. I learned to begin each day with a totally different attitude, one that included humility and an open heart.

I'm no Bible preaching geek. I'm pretty cool, hopefully respected and loved by people that are in my life. But I select those people far more carefully now. I learned how to take off the mask that I hid behind for so long and got real with myself and God. I no longer needed to get even with the "Buddy's" of the world. I no longer needed to prove I was somebody. God accepts me with all my flaws and shortcomings. That, in itself, makes me somebody. He answered each and every one of my prayers. He has never let me down. I got tested and sometimes I fell short, but I got right back up and looked forward to the next challenge.

CHAPTER 6

Life's Lesson

I TRULY BELIEVE THAT I have been blessed with a great family. Even with all of our "quirks." I have come to accept that everything happens for a reason, and each situation in which we find ourselves provides a valuable lesson that can be used for our eventual growth. I love my family with all my heart, mind, body and soul. I understand how fortunate I have been that, during my incarceration, my family stood by me. My cousins on my mom's side kept in touch with me throughout my bid. Quite honestly, I was surprised by that. None of them were ever "in trouble" and each of them went on to college. Most have now graduated and have begun their adult lives. Mind you, I have always been the black sheep of the family, and all my cousins led very sheltered lives, probably because of me. Prison is the last place you would ever expect to see any of them. But throughout the years they showed their love and support for me. They would write to me often, and visit me a few times a year. At Christmas they all contributed money and bought me a Christmas present. But I have to say I was most surprised by my cousin, Andy, and what he said to me one time when he visited me.

At each visit, Andy would ask the same question, "So, Mike, what kind of plans do you have when you get home"? Quite honestly, in 2008, my "plans" were still corrupt. I still had hidden agendas. I was still on the scam, hustling the life. It was still the "Life Times a Million" attitude. I would have all kinds of great ideas with one idea more outrageous than the next. I have always had a very creative mind and I can get pretty excited about my visions. Most people can't see what I am able to envision. That's okay, they don't have to.

When my cousins came home for Christmas break, they came to visit me. Again, Andy asked the same question. Mind you, my Dad had passed away by this time. So when Andy asked what my plans were, I told him that, "I was going to conquer the world. I had new visions with modified ideas." And, that's when it happened. Andy said, "You know, Michael, your mother has always supported you and she's tired now and instead of coming home and spending everyone's money, why don't you just get a job at McDonald's or go to work at the bakery?" What did he just say? I thought, first off, Andy, I might work at a McDonalds or a bakery, but the one thing you don't seem to get is I would *own* the McDonald's or the bakery and I would hire you to be the baker!

I was angry because I felt disrespected. I was hurt by the implication that I should settle for a low-paying job because that was the most I could hope for. But it made me wonder about how many other people might think this same way. I acknowledge the fact that I will always be a former inmate with a violent felony on my record. But, you know, I am not worried about that and if I had accepted Andy's comment I would never have been able to grow as a person. How many people get side-lined by other people's opinions? I swallowed my pride that day and let the comment go unanswered. But I have to admit, it was one of the lowest points in my incarceration.

However, there was another other time that topped this low point in my self-esteem. This piece of "humble pie" really put things into perspective for me. One morning, I woke up and my knee was twice its size. In prison, you have to be on death's door before you see a doctor. Simply put, I needed an MRI on my knee. As worried as I was about my knee, I was also excited because that meant I had to go to the hospital. In other words, field trip! Any excuse to see beyond the fence is considered a really big day. This one particular morning I was notified by the C.O. that I had to be ready by 8:30 a.m. because I was going to be taken to the hospital for the MRI. I drank my morning coffee, and by 8:15 a.m. I was getting processed for the trip. Then, I was shackled hands to waist and waist to ankles. Even though my leg hurt as I hopped to the van, I was thrilled to be leaving the prison if only for a short time.

We arrived at the hospital and all eyes were on me since I am covered in green from head to foot and I am in shackles. As I was checked in by the nurse, she offered a cup of coffee. I thought she had included me and answered, "Thank you, Miss; I would love a cup of coffee." That is when she glared at me and said, "You can't have coffee." Then she walked away.

I had never had an MRI before so I had no idea what to expect. For 30 minutes I listened to the noisiest jackhammer sound I ever heard. When I finally was let out of the "tube" I felt really sick. My stomach hurt and I was light headed. Nobody cared how I felt. I just got re-shackled and transported back to the van. Half jokingly I said to one of the transporters, "Hey, what do you recommend, from Mickey D's--a double cheeseburger or chicken sandwich"? He asked me how long it had been since I had eaten at McDonald's. I answered, "At least five years, sir." So we departed the hospital and out of nowhere we pulled into a McDonald's. I felt like a kid at Christmas! But, instead of going to McDonald's we pulled around to the back to a bagel shop. Okay, a bagel is just fine with me. Then they took turns going in the shop. Before I knew it, I was trapped in the back seat like a dog watching his owners eat their lunch. The only difference between me and a dog was that the dog at least would get the scraps. All I could do was sit back and talk to Jesus thanking Him for giving me this experience. I thought back to how I had been raised. How many times had my Dad bought lunch for all the guys on the crew? If he ate, everyone ate. I continued talking to Jesus for the rest of the way back to Mid-State. I thanked him for giving me another reason why I would never live like this again. I just ask Him to help me learn from this experience and to help me to always remember how disregarded I felt.

So remembering how I felt that day, I replayed Andy's words over and over again in my mind. I thought long and hard about what he had said and why he said it. Here was my younger cousin who was once at the top of my list but who had now sunk to the bottom. I thought the world of him. I was really bothered by what he said and didn't understand how he could have said it. Then I came up with the answer.

The average inmate allows a prison bid to cripple him for life. He never grows from the experience. The experience paralyzes him so all he can do is drain the State for benefits and Social Security insurance and basically lives off the system for the rest of his life. Then there are others who feel that once you have been a convicted criminal you are forever considered to be a lowly and worthless individual whose only hope for the future is to work at a very low paying job.

Listen to me! Everyone has a chance for success. No matter how bad my situation was, I knew my life was far from over. In fact, my true life was just beginning. I did wrong and I paid for my wrong with years of my life.

The day I had to appear for the extortion charge, I gave myself to God. I promised if he helped me get through that, I would change my life. I know what you are thinking, "Oh, boy here we go. Guess what, he went to prison and he found God. He took a college course and now he is going to get his life turned around." How many times do we hear that stereotypical scene play out in the news? The sad reality is it doesn't work for everyone. But, it does work for many and with His help I will be one of the successes. If God promises a life filled with rewards and happiness, then my life must be worth living! Christ died on the cross to forgive us our sins—*all of them*. That, plus a prison sentence, puts me even.

My cousins went to college to pursue their dreams and I'm very proud of them for graduating and reaching their goals. However, everyone must learn in their own way. Now, I do not recommend a prison bid as an "educational avenue," but prison was my University of Hard Knocks and I graduated with honors. This was the experience that gave me an opportunity for a brand new life pursuit. Prison gave me more than any college in the world could have offered me. It was my time away from home, my life-altering experience that taught me the lessons I desperately needed to learn. I needed to be stripped of all possessions, all identity. I needed time to overcome addiction; to be knocked down off of my high horse. I was so tired of always going against the grain. I needed to be saved from myself. I had lost my soul! I desperately needed time to search for and reclaim it from the devil, himself.

If you think doing time is easy, think again. It's an almost impossible task, especially for guys who really are attempting to take advantage of the time and change their lives. They say it's cool being the tough guy. Well, in prison, the truly "tough guys" are those who can face their demons and do something about them. This has been the greatest challenge of my entire life. I can't compare it with anything I've ever been through. To say it "nicely," the state prison system is the master mind twist. But, it can work if you learn how to let it work for you. There isn't a chance that I will let this experience hold me back. I've come too far. I certainly did not spend all these years dreaming of flipping hamburgers at McDonald's.

Today, I am no longer angry with Andy. Actually, I have to give him thanks for giving me the extra push and determination to do the right thing especially when no one except God was looking. It was the rebirth of my self-respect and the planting of the seeds of honor and integrity.

All dreams are worth pursuing. Don't ever let fear get in your way and don't let someone's opinion misdirect you. Follow your heart because it is controlled by God. If you take nothing else from reading my story, take this...*don't ever sell yourself short!*

CHAPTER 7

The Road Leading Home

LEARNING ABOUT SELF-RESPECT HAS BEEN my biggest hurdle. Comprehending the meaning of self-respect was exceptionally hard for me. I couldn't describe it and I couldn't remember a time when I had it. How can one begin to respect others, if he doesn't know how to respect himself? In my past life, I poisoned my body with drugs, cigarettes and alcohol. I was a male prostitute. How I didn't contract any venereal diseases was a miracle in itself. I may have beaten those odds but I recognized that I was running out of time. I had no more time for mistakes and bad choices. I could no longer claim to be young and stupid. The time I had to use those excuses was all used up.

I still have the two bullets inside me from the shooting. At the time, it was too dangerous to attempt to remove them because of where they were located. But they serve as a daily reminder that I could have very easily died that day. My life could have ended at a very early age. Those bullets are all the proof I need to understand just how precious life is.

For whatever reason, that day God said it wasn't my time. I think about that every day and value every minute. I've learned how to respect life in general.

When I visited my Dad the night before he died, he set my future course. His big concern was for the family. He told me to watch out for my brothers, to always be there for my Mom and to never forget Janet. He made me promise him that I would do all of those things. Before I had to leave he said to me, "Michael, learn everything you're supposed to learn, finish your time and become the man you were destined to be." That was basically the same thing the judge said to me. I've carried that inside me for all these years. I had to become a man. Men didn't do the things I did. They didn't think about themselves first before anyone else like I had done for so long. My Dad has been gone for over four years and his words remain etched in my heart. He didn't give me an option and it doesn't matter whether I think I'm ready or not. Men "man up," and do the things that need to be done.

When deciding which of the two IPA jobs I would take, the choice was easy. I knew that Dad wanted me to be the happiest guy in the world. And that's when I said, "Okay, enough. I'm not mad at God any more, Dad. I'm not mad that you're not here with me. It's okay and I will become a man and I'm starting today." So, I start each day asking God for protection and strength for my journey through life and to always keep watch over me and my family. Today I smile all day long. If you were to ask me why I'd tell you it's because it's okay to smile. That happy-go-lucky little boy that disappeared so long ago has finally re-appeared as a grown man.

I will always remember this one guy that came to the MICA unit. His first day in the program he walked in and he reminded me of a deformed camel. His back was completely hunched and twisted-looking. The only way I know how to describe his shape is to say he looked mangled. You almost felt sorry for him just by the way he looked. I would watch him brush his teeth in the morning and it was pathetic. His head would be buried in the sink. Never once did he look up in the mirror. I would say things like, "Joe, pick up your head, look in the mirror. Tell yourself that the sky is the limit." I kept at him every day for I don't know how long. Little by little he started to recognize his existence. I was relentless in feeding him positive energy. He couldn't look at himself in the mirror because he, too, had lost his self-respect. He told me that he felt worthless. You have to find your self-worth and hold on to it for dear life. I am so proud of him and I can tell you today, he is a role model in the world of recovery. What a comeback.

Each and every morning I look in the mirror and say, "Good morning, God, good morning, Michael." I can look in the mirror because I can see the image looking back at me has purpose in his life. I am a new man. My prison experience changed my life. I was sent to prison for one reason and that was so I could save my life. The time away was devastating in so many ways. It was all the years of growing pains that I never experienced as a kid all rolled into one.

When I found out about the Limited Time Credit Allowance Law, I saw the opportunity and there wasn't anything that was going to stop me from earning the early release—well, anything that I had control over. In a place of little hope, this was finally one ray of light. When Father Weber said, "Tell Michael it's time to come home…God is waiting for him," I ran with my arms wide open. The IPA position in the MICA-ASAT dorm was more than just a job--it turned out to be a way of life for me.

I've said before, things in the state change really fast. One day it is like this and the next it is completely different—"What is up is down, and what is down is up." Nothing proves this like the listings for the IPA positions that kept changing minute by minute. If you remember, the Chapel job could no longer be used for LTCA requirement. At that time, I wasn't too worried because I also had the MICA-ASAT position to fall back on. Well, guess what other position the State downgraded? You guessed it—the MICA dorm IPA!

When the state decided that my job no longer qualified as an IPA position I was heartsick! Actually, I was devastated because it threatened my early release that I had worked so hard on for two full years. Secondly, I felt that the program gave me an incredible way to give back to a community of people that needed so much. In this position, I was the all-hours guy to go to. When guys had seizures in the middle of the program, I was the one who saw them off to the hospital. In the middle of the night when guys would get paranoid and needed someone there, it was me they ran to. When anyone had a problem I was the first line of defense. And now, the state didn't think that position met the requirements.

Faced with the distinct possibility that getting out early wasn't going to be on the table, I didn't know what to do. I asked Ms. D. how could this happen? What does it mean? How could the work I had done for the last two years not count? When Ms. D. had to tell me that effective immediately I was out of an IPA job, we both were at a loss for words. But, Ms. D. was on the phone in five seconds. She contacted Mrs. Leonard who was the Educational Supervisor to ask if there was a chance she would hire me as a teacher's aide so that I could continue in the LTCA program. As it worked out, the teacher's aide position was now the only position at Mid-State that qualified for the LTCA program. I was able to interview with Mrs. Leonard that afternoon. I already knew her because she was the person who approved of my college courses. So when I went to the interview she was more than understanding and hired me on the spot. I couldn't say, "Thank you, Jesus" loud enough. So I was able to continue on my quest through a series of different jobs. I never left the Church job or the MICA position. But now, I was a volunteer. I couldn't walk away from that bunch of crazy guys and I absolutely could not stay away from the Church.

I have to say, the combination of all of my jobs was an enormous educational advantage. I became an aide to a teacher who taught me so much about technology like the Kindle Fire and the Nook. I had absolutely no idea these things existed. We also spent time comparing recipes. With both of us coming from Italian backgrounds, cooking and eating was second nature to us. I thought things were finally back on track.

Next thing I knew, I was being called to my Counselor's office –again. I was told that my name had just popped up on the computer and I could put my application in to New York State to review my case and make a determination whether they will give me the early release. I couldn't swallow. I suddenly didn't know what to do. Here I was worried sick that the state would throw out my application altogether and now I actually have to submit it.

I said, "Ms. D. I think we should wait another month because on March 8th, I will complete my two years of college work and we might need that for back up." See, the state is entirely based on a number system. Everything is numbers and the numbers have to match up. She agreed and I left her office thinking I knew how we would proceed. That night I went down to the Law Library to print out an application and review the law just to make sure I had all my ducks in a row. There was no room for mistakes. This was a one time and one time only opportunity. I came away feeling as though everything checked out—at least on my end.

Two days later, Ms. D. called me back down to her office and said that I had to sign the application. What? She said that she reviewed it with the other four counselors and they felt that it was time to send the application off. I told her that I didn't think we should rush it. I had worked so long and hard for this day and now that it was actually here, I froze. She said, "No, you have to sign it now. Sign right here, Mr. Tandoi." I said a silent prayer asking God to take the paper and deliver me from the chains of prison. Then, I signed the application and the numbers game started.

Each and every required signature had a time limit. Ms. D. had 24 hours to get the application to the Senior Counselor for signature. Then another 24 hours for the Department of Programs to sign off; then the Superintendent/Captain. Only if it passed all the approvals from the facility would it then get sent to the New York State Capital in Albany for the final review. Albany only had two weeks once they received the application to act. If Albany approved the application, it then went to the Commissioner of Prisons who had 24 hours to sign it. Oh, my God!

I didn't know how I was going to wait through all of this time. The only thing I could do at this point was pray. I prayed and prayed and prayed. I poured myself into my Bible studies. Every day I read the Magnificat and sang every hymn I knew. Then I had to leave it in God's hands.

On Tuesday, January 17, 2012, Ms. D. let me know that the application had left the prison and it was on its way to Albany. I asked her when exactly did it leave the prison and she said, January 13th. Of all the days this vitally important paper had to race across the state, it was on my father's birthday. I was overjoyed and I knew that my Dad had a hand in making this happen.

Well, that joy lasted two days. That is when Ms. D. called me down for another one of those talks that started out with, "Don't start worrying, yet..." You see the state had contacted the facility and wanted to know how I was getting credit for the IPA work when these programs were not IPA programs. Wait just a second! They were when I took them and because of no fault of mine they were cut from the list. I should still get the credit, right?

Apparently, the woman from the state had agreed with my counselor after she had explained the situation and the Mid-State Senior Counselor had also spoken to the people in Albany. It was left at, "Well, I understand he did the work, but I don't know if he can be grandfathered in." That's when Ms. D. went to Plan B—college work. Well, Mrs. Leonard no longer worked at the facility and the substitute principal didn't know the whole situation. When she faxed my college work into the State, she only sent in one-year from Penn Foster for Business Management and didn't know about the second year at Ohio University for Sociology.

After that, I received a letter from our Department of Programs that basically terminated my college participation because the state said that Penn Foster College wasn't accredited!!! I was sick to my stomach. Before I had signed up for the courses, I had checked the college out in the Department of Education Training Handbook and the educational supervisor for Mid-State signed off on the course. What are they talking about?

I've seen this kind of scenario happen so many times with other inmates. When something was right the state made it wrong and vice versa—always changing the rules. Please, God, don't let this be. I was holding it together as best as I could but we were out of time on my application. Everyone was out of time. Judgment Day was at hand!

The night I got the letter from the Department of Programs I also received another piece of mail from the State. I thought it was the letter I had been waiting for. I ran to my room, prayed before I opened it. This time I found that I had received a reduction on my parole due to a request I had submitted in October, 2011. My post supervision (parole) was supposed to be for five years, and it had now been reduced to only three years because there was an error in my original sentencing. This was great news, but not the news I had been praying for. I couldn't fully appreciate the reduction in parole because of the stress in my heart over the early release. Looking back I have to say that I did a great job of not losing my mind through all of that.

On January 31, 2012, I woke up at 6 a.m. and started to read from my special prayer book given to me by Father Weber. After reading from the prayer book, I read my daily prayers from the Magnificat, then two chapters from the Bible. After that, I listened to The Christian Radio station and my favorite religious song was playing, The Our Father. At 7 a.m., I went to breakfast and was back in the unit at 7:15 a.m. I had to wait until 8 a.m. before I could move to the morning program in the Chapel. At 7:55 a.m. the C.O.s phone rang and my heart jumped because I just knew that phone call was for me. "Tandoi", the C.O. yelled, "Before you go to the Chapel run over to Building 3, Mrs. DiBraccio wants to see you." Oh, no. This is it. It's now or never. There is no tomorrow. It was 8 a.m. and movement started and I made my way to Building 3. On the way I spoke to God. "All right, God, I'm ready, let's do this; either way, if I get this or not, I'm still with you." I entered the building, checked in with the C.O. and took a seat. Ms. D. appeared in the doorway with papers in her hands. She called me to enter the office. We both said our good mornings and she slid the papers across the table to me. I asked, "Ms. DiBraccio is this the decision?" "Yes, Mr. Tandoi, it is." I couldn't look, I just couldn't look. At least at this moment there was still a chance to hope. Once I looked at the papers there would be no more hope, there would only be the decision. I silently spoke to God one more time and then I looked down at the papers. There it was—my LTCA had come through and my new release date was August 23, 2012. The relief was overwhelming. I dropped to my knees because my legs gave way. And on my knees, I praised God.

Through all the ups and downs of the "waiting" time, Reverend Ellis reminded me that God's time is perfect always. He said, "God has to make sure all the tumblers are aligned so that the safe can be opened up." I was the safe and God unlocked the door to my freedom.

After all my years of incarceration, I was almost at a loss as to how to react to the reality that I would be going home within months—no longer years. You dream of this day from the very first day you're processed. I thought when I got to less than 90 days I would just ride out the time. But, it didn't work like that. I lived in a mental health dorm. Even though I wasn't the IPA anymore, I was still living there and was still the go-to guy.

It was now getting into summer and when the weather gets warmer, things start to get even crazier than usual. The heat really affects some inmates especially if they're on medication. Their individual problems are still problems only bigger. Additionally, I watched as guys got "hit" at the parole board which means they will sit around for another year or two until their case would be reviewed by the board again.

There is one guy that I've known for over three years. He's been here for over 20 years. He committed a murder in the 1980s. He hasn't had any luck in the last eight times he has been to parole. Since his sentence was for life, the parole board can legally hold him for all his life. I often wondered how some of these guys made it through 20, 30, 40 years in prison without losing their minds. I know each and every one of us made our own destiny and we have to live with the consequences, but when you live with these men, even murderers, rapists, drug addicts, etc, all of our pasts get blurred. We all become just guys who live in a dorm. Well, this guy took the last parole meeting really hard. Ms. D. refers to it as "decomposition." I call it a meltdown of the brain and you start doing things that you normally would not do. For starters, he walked in front of a group of 46 inmates, two counselors, and a C.O. with a six-inch "banger"(any object that could be used as weapon) accusing someone from the group of putting the banger on his bed. He started leaving crazy notes all around the house and patrolling the unit at 3:00 a.m. None of this was making sense. I felt really bad for him because I knew he was digging himself a hole from which he would not be able to climb out.

It was a Saturday morning, waffle day at Mid-State. I was on my way to breakfast when the C.O. called me into the office to tell me that this guy was going to be moved off of the unit. I asked where he was and the C.O. said he went to breakfast. Well, he never went to breakfast. He turned around and went back to his room. I went to look for him. His body normally shakes all the time and he talks with his hands flying wildly. Additionally, he is a "cutter"—that means that he has hundreds of blade marks up and down his arms. When he gets nervous, the shaking is even worse. So, when I found him, I tried to calm him down because I knew how he could get. I could see that he was trying to get attention because he had to do something to stop the move to the other unit. As I was trying to talk to him, he stopped me mid-sentence and said, "Tandoi, I'm tired of this life. It hurts too much and I wish that the God you talk about would just end my life." Then he grabbed the razor and told me I had two options: "You can leave my room and give me a couple of minutes to do what I have to do, or you can get some body bags because I'm taking a couple of these guys with me." I said to him, "Bro, that's not fair, I can't let you do this, and I can't watch you hurt yourself or anybody else." As I was talking to him I tried to get the razor out of his hands but that wasn't going to happen.

I didn't realize that the C.O. was on rounds, but all of a sudden there he was in the room with us. The C.O. said to him as cool as possible, "Listen, I have always respected you and I really like you. I want you to do the right thing. Let's get to the bottom of this and let's get you the right help." The C.O. was able to calm him down enough and the transport team was called. They arrived and cuffed him and took him to the health observation unit. After three days, he was moved to his new unit. So in the end, no one got hurt. But, that is how crazy it can get in a matter of minutes.

Instead of preparing to leave, I found myself feeling anxious about the few remaining months I had left. I began to pray for extra angels and saints to watch over me. "Please, Lord, protect me and get me home to my family." By this time I had only 35 days left to go, I wasn't sleeping at night. I think my sleep was disturbed because I was having a hard time deciding how I would say goodbye. Most guys just leave, run for the gate and are never heard from again. I knew I needed more closure. This has been my "home" for half of a decade. Saying goodbye to this "family" of crazy guys and the staff is so bittersweet. Then, adding to these feelings of melancholia is the fact that Father Weber would say goodbye to Mid-State a couple of weeks before I left.

He had just received a promotion to Head Chaplain for the New York State Prison Department. He would be relocated in the central office in Albany. He had been at Mid-State for 28 years. I was so happy for him and I was looking forward to "praying him out." I told him just because he is leaving Mid-State doesn't mean that I won't be contacting him. I am one of his sheep! I will never forget that he was responsible for helping me make the transition to recovery. I knew I would sincerely miss him.

I think in some odd way, preparing to leave has been the hardest part of my prison bid. This has been my daily life for quite a while. I had to make my way through the really tough times. I had to overcome the old Michael. In a strange way, there is a small piece of me that is sad and I feel a bit overwhelmed with the thought of "starting over." This is the day

I've been praying for. The day I can go home to my family. My prayers have been answered. So why do I feel this way?

I've overcome harder things than this, so I had to figure out how to get past these feelings that are, well, confusing. So, I spent my time giving away my belongings. There is a type of prison "code." When you come to a state prison you come with nothing. And, when you leave, the code says you leave with very little. You might have your personal paperwork, pictures, etc. but only the really important things get taken. Whatever you may have accumulated during your years—clothing, shoes, books, etc. you pass on to others. None of us have anything, but some of us *really* don't have anything. I gave my winter blanket to a guy from Rochester, because I knew he could really use a warm blanket. Some of these guys don't have family support so they are in a real need of basic things, like a blanket. I gave away my two "dress" shirts to a friend who I know will wear them on school days because he is trying to get his GED. It made me happy to know I was passing on my things to guys who had a genuine need for them. I've been told that it's bad luck to take your things home when you leave. I'm not sure if I believe that theory because some of these guys only have what they have here. So leaving it behind would be really difficult for them.

From being so busy that you don't know how to get everything done in a day to not having a job was hard for me. I no longer worked as the education aide because now I was in the transition program which was supposed to prepare us for re-entry into society. I really liked the instructor and I remember the day we talked about financial credit. I was glued to what he had to say. He was also an inmate and one of my friends. He had worked on Wall Street for years and owned a business. He had some great information that was really helpful to me. Re-establishing my credit is an important goal for me. It won't be easy, but it is something I will have to do.

Part of transition included a lot of time working out in the gym. Because the Recreation Department was in the same building as the chapel, I was very familiar with the area and the people that worked in the department. I felt as much at home in the gym as I did in the chapel. In June, I started working out in earnest. What I mean by that is I have worked out from time to time but I was never really dedicated or disciplined enough to be very successful. But a major part of my recovery was spent in regaining my health. Alcohol, drugs and cigarettes are not exactly a recipe for a healthy lifestyle. I have been playing softball and soccer for most of the time in prison, but in central New York, you don't play sports in the snow. So there is a good part of the year where you are fairly inactive.

One day, in the gym, I noticed this guy lifting weights. I noticed him because he actually seemed to know what he was doing. I asked him if I could join him and that workout was the most intense workout I have ever had. I was really impressed with his knowledge and dedication to the program. The next day, I offered him a jar of protein powder from the commissary once every two weeks if he would train me until it was time for me to leave prison. He agreed and I worked out with him faithfully for my last three months. I got yelled at on a daily basis because I'm a talker. If it only took talking to gain muscle mass I would be known as the "rock."

On my nights off, when I wasn't playing sports, jogging or working out, I usually met with two of my best friends, Mike and Joe, out in the yard. When Craig and Nicky were still here (they had been released by this time) we made up the Five Musketeers. We were a band of brothers—Craig, Nicky, Mike, Joe and me. The truth is we knew more about each other than we did of our real brothers. We were surrogate family members to each other.

Mike and I had been together since 2007. He was my very first prison brother. Mike is my Italian pal. We latched on to each other from the first time we met. When either of us would receive visits from family members, we made sure we got introduced to the other's family. In prison, if you get introduced to family members it means that you are considered a close friend. Mike had a tough bid. He is a father of three beautiful kids—one boy and two girls. His youngest daughter was born when he was in prison and I was honored to be named as her godfather. That's how close we became.

Joe and I have been together since 2008. One night Joe was telling me how much his time was going to change once I left. We had spent hours upon hours talking about inventions and how all we needed to do was to invent just one thing that the world really needed. Then we would produce the item and sell it around the world. Joe and I both imagined ourselves in a new life. Joe has big plans for his return and they are all legal. We never wasted one minute talking about nonsense. I can't wait to be re-united with these guys. I will miss truly them.

At the 21 day count, Mrs. N. yelled my name along with, J.J., another inmate. We both went to the bubble to see what she wanted. She told us that "ID" had called and after lunch we were to go down and take our going home pictures. I jumped up and the biggest smile went across my face. I remember watching other inmates go for their ID pictures and feeling so envious. But now I get to go, how awesome is this?

At ID, the C.O. called my name and that is when it happened, again…my face lit up like a Christmas tree. After a couple of questions she took my picture. Actually, she had to take two pictures because in the first one, I looked Asian because my smile was so big that it caused my eyes to almost close shut. When J.J. finished, she wished us good luck and we walked back to the dorm together. At one point on our walk we stopped, looked at each other and said, "Well, it's official now. We're going home!" J.J. left three days before me.

I was now down to the last three weeks before I would leave. I knew that plans were in the works for some kind of going away bash. I had no idea what it would be. The big boss at the Department of Programs shot down the pizza party and the ice cream party. She said, "Out of the question." I continued to get daily requests for my "stuff." I was taking a sip of coffee when a friend of mine, who has been down longer that I have been alive, asked if I could leave him my coffee cup. I said, "It's yours and

I will even give you my left over coffee and my coffee filter." Years ago, I had made the coffee filter out of a handkerchief and a Kool-Aid top. He seemed really pleased and so was I.

As each day passed, I still had moments of anxiety. There was one night that I wanted to lock myself in my locker, but chose against it. I don't know what actually triggered this feeling but I think it was a combination of a lot of things. For starters, July 26 was the ninth anniversary of the day I was shot. It also turned out to be the same day my Mom and Aunt Bon had an appointment with Father Ray Fleming, in Rochester. I asked them to set up an appointment for me on my first day home. I really felt I needed to be blessed by a priest the minute I got home. I didn't know Father Ray but my Mom did and ironically, St. Monica's Church is just a few blocks away from the corner on which I got shot. I wonder if God has plans for me in this neighborhood.

Along with this date being a kind of anniversary, for some reason I felt the prison system closing in on me. I thought the C.O.s were out to get me and would somehow steal my going home date. There was no specific reason for my paranoia and the C.O.s didn't do anything different that night. It was me. I thought I was going to lose it, but somehow I was able to overcome the feeling of dread.

To top things off, we lost our softball game that night—the first and only loss of the season. I had played softball for all my years in prison. Again, playing sports is considered living a healthy lifestyle so participation in sports is encouraged. This year I was nominated to be Captain of the Mid-State All Stars. Sounds great, right? Well, in all honesty, I had been praying like crazy for the last three weeks especially because of the softball series. This may sound unusual but in prison all sports are serious. So serious that people get hurt all the time. In addition to being named Captain, I am also the pitcher and my team has won five straight Championships. With only a short time left, I was faced with a hard decision. Play or not to play because when someone gets injured in prison it can stop your release date until you are well again.

So, I was scheduled to pitch the all star game against the Prison Saints which is a team that comes into the prison from New Jersey. This team is made up of civilians from the streets but let me tell you, they are the best softball players I have ever played. They go from prison to prison and beat just about every team they play against. In 2010, they came here and blew us away. They actually had "equipment" including titanium bats, which was no match for us. The softballs get hit so hard it's like dodging bullets. Once there was a line drive that almost took off my head. So going into this game was a big worry for me. I knew I wanted to play for Mid-State but it was a high risk. So I had prayed everyday for three weeks leading up to the series. "Lord, please protect me and the team. Let us have a safe game with no injuries on either side and please, Lord, don't let me take a line drive up the middle that I can't handle. Amen."

On game day, I started out the day at the gym. During my workout, I heard God say to me, "Don't worry, Michael. Go out there tonight and have fun. I am with you and won't let anything happen." So that is what I did. I trusted God would keep me safe. I swear it was one of the greatest games I ever played for several reasons. To start off, before the game, the guys let me say a prayer asking for safety and a win. I asked God to keep the team together, let us hit the gaps and play great baseball. That was exactly what happened. I did pitch a great game, but everyone hit, got on base and came into home. We were playing a team that usually caught every ball that ever went into the air. But in the end we won! Not only did we win this game but we won the 2012 Championship, too. In fact, the team we played against in the Championship, the Tigers, threw up the flag of defeat and walked off the field. 23-4 was the final score. Over all the years I was in prison, our team of misfits won five Championships in Softball, two Championships in Soccer and three Super Bowls in football. This season, especially, will stay with me forever.

July 28, 2012 was Father Weber's last Saturday night Mass, and I had to come up with a plan for a memorable service. I wrote a letter to Father and wanted to read it at the service. On the Wednesday before the service

I asked Father to call the civilians from our REC (Resident Encounters with Christ) Weekends and invite them to the service. Father thought that was a good idea and he made the calls. Saturday night's Mass was the most beautiful and meaningful Mass ever. The Church was packed. I wasn't planning on serving that night but as it turned out, I did. I was glad because I got to sit next to the man who had shepherd me through all the pain and trials of my incarceration. In the letter that I read, I told Father that I loved him like a son loves a father. I did break down, just a little. Father seemed touched by my words and I felt great that I had the opportunity to tell him how much he had influenced my recovery. As a surprise, Father Weber bought us the biggest cake we've ever seen. Cake and coffee after the service was truly the icing on a great event. That night will be one of my best memories of prison.

August 17, I was notified that I had received a package from my Mom. I loved getting packages. But this one was like Christmas and my birthday all rolled into one. This was a package of going home clothes! My Mom said she sent a pair of jeans, a shirt and a belt—*a belt!* I didn't have any street clothes so here was one more item that got checked off the going home list. I wouldn't be able to receive or open the package until August 23, going home day!

I woke up Thursday, August 23, at 5:30 a.m. There was excitement but there was also a sense of peace. I didn't feel like I had to hurry so I read my prayers from my special prayer book. I read from the Magnificat and a few verses from the Bible. Then I did 800 push-ups. This morning began just like so many others with one exception. Today was the day I was going home!

It was actually time for me to leave, time to say good bye to some of the people I will never forget and will always consider my real friends, the ones that I can count on my hand. Most guys I've seen on their last days just run for the gate. No goodbyes are said. I just wanted to take in the sight of my room one last time. I wanted to walk slowly past the C.O.'s desk, past the community room where I cooked my "Tando-licious" meals, attended programs, listened to all those talks, watched TV and just sat with my fellow inmates for so many years. The C.O. said, "Mr. Tandoi, it's time to go. Good luck to you and don't ever let me see your face in here again." I smiled and said, "Yes, Sir." Then it was time for me to get processed—for the last time. It was time for "movement" so Josh, Kenny, Joey and John walked me part of the way to the front gate, a place I had never been. We hugged and wished each other well and said we would see each other again. We promised we wouldn't forget the time we had spent together. I never expected that I would be choked up when I had to leave them behind, but I was.

During processing, I was given the package with my street clothes and I changed out of my prison greens. It felt so strange to feel the tightness of the jeans and the belt around my waist compared to my greens with the drawstring waist. Strange as it felt, it felt great. Once I got changed it was time for me to walk to the gate house.

The gatekeeper unlocked the first lock and the gate swung open. There were two other inmates leaving that day and we walked together though the gate to the outside and toward the secondary gate. Before the second gate would be unlocked, the one behind us had to shut and lock with a loud industrial slam. Then another locking device opened the secondary gate and the door swung free. For a minute, I froze. I didn't know if I should step out or not. My Mom, Chuck and brother, Vito, were there to meet me. I just kept my eyes on them and stepped forward. I had to walk to them because they were not allowed any closer to me. Then the reality set in…I was free. Free of the gates, free to breathe again.

I know deep in my heart that God didn't save me just so my life could be spared. I know he has other plans for me. I'm not entirely sure what those plans might be, but I'm ready for them. My life wasn't exactly a fairytale, textbook story, but through my experiences maybe, just maybe I will be able to help someone find their strength to overcome their demons. At least, that is what I hope will happen.

CHAPTER 8

Home at Last

THE TRANSITION BACK INTO EVERYDAY life was much more of an adjustment than I ever thought it would be. On the ride home from Mid-State, I was like a kid in a candy store. Everything looked so good—so new. It had been three years since I took the trip to see my Dad and that day I cried most of the way. But this time I was wide-eyed and couldn't take in the sights fast enough. So much had changed. New commercial buildings, restaurants and housing developments now stood where only vacant land used to be. This ride home went a lot faster than that last one did, too and it even included a stop at McDonald's for a double cheeseburger.

When I got back to Rochester, I immediately reported to Parole, met with my parole officer and got my "rules to live by." I am not allowed to drive and I must be home by 8 p.m. every evening and, of course, no drugs or alcohol. Next, I went to see Father Ray at St. Monica's. He welcomed me home and said that he was happy to finally meet me. Then he brought me into the church and there he anointed me with holy oil. By this time my anxiety level had lessened and I was beginning to feel safe again. I listened to the silence of the Church as I breathed in the smells; the candle wax, the incense, the wood of the pews. I don't know if this will become my church home or not, but at this moment I could feel God's welcoming arms around me.

During the next few days, I met with family and friends, some of whom I hadn't seen in almost six years. They could see that I was different and I could sense that they weren't sure how to react when they saw me. It was a strange feeling for me, too. My mother and Chuck had prepared a room for me in their home, a room with an actual door, my very own door. It was surprising to realize just how much I had missed all those "normal" things like doors, private bathrooms and, of course, freedom.

I got home on a Thursday and that Saturday we had a memorial service for my Dad at the cemetery. It was a beautiful summer's day in August; sunny with a bright blue sky and wispy white clouds. My cousins, Gene and Janice, picked me up and we arrived at the cemetery before anyone else had gotten there and I was really glad I would have a few minutes alone with my Dad. As we turned into the cemetery a lump got caught in my throat and it caught me off guard. Then reality hit me, oh God, this is where my father is. As I was led to the gravesite, I was overcome by the loss. I had cried an ocean of tears when I was told of my father's passing, but I didn't deal with any of the funeral or burial customs because I wasn't here. I didn't have the honor of walking my Dad to his resting place. I didn't have the opportunity to feel his name engraved in the cold gray stone. I had felt the loss, but I didn't have the occasion to stand with my family and grieve. I didn't leave him with that one last rose.

Family members and friends arrived a few at a time and I was able to spend a few minutes with each of them. They all hugged me and said they were happy that I was finally home. Then I caught sight of my

Uncle Tweedy. He reached out for me and as he put his arms around me, I could feel his weight as I seemed to hold him up as I hugged him back. He had aged in the last six years and his rugged face seemed deeply etched with sadness. As he hugged me he whispered, "I miss him so much."

Father Ray officiated at the memorial service and then he announced that I would say a few words. I spoke about how it was the time for us to come together as my Dad would have wanted. I told everyone how grateful I was to be back with them and how much I had missed them. I promised that I would live my life with honor though God's help. My brothers and I each wrote a brief message on a balloon and we closed the ceremony by launching the balloon toward Heaven, toward my Dad. Although the day was harder than I anticipated, it was exactly as I had hoped it would have been. It was a joyous day filled with deep emotion and love from all those who attended the ceremony.

The following Monday I started working for Chuck in his asphalt company. It felt good to get back to something that was so familiar to me. It really was like "riding a bike." Even the oily smell of the asphalt brought back memories—good memories. But after a few weeks, I found I was almost ready to quit. That would have been the very first time of all my working years that I ever considered throwing in the towel. I felt I was still incarcerated, I felt my hands and legs were still shackled. I was still dealing with petty jealousy just like the snitch notes in prison. You see, Chuck has a son and daughter who I consider to be my step brother and sister. They are both part of Chuck's business. I can understand that they might feel somewhat threatened by me because I do have years of experience running a very successful asphalt business. They may even think that I want to push my way into their business. But there is absolutely no truth to that. They might even be concerned that their father could get hurt by misplacing his trust in me. I could understand all of that but I had to figure out a way to show them that I didn't want their business and I wasn't a threat to any of them. I just wanted a chance to make a life for myself. Anyway, this one particular day, Chuck's son had been riding me so hard that I ended up telling him off. Fifteen minutes later I apologized to him. I didn't want to create a barrier between us. Then it happened, I was sent out to complete a job with my own paving crew. I did such a good job that I not only impressed Chuck but his daughter, too, who was the office manager for the company. They were so pleased that they gave me my own asphalt crew. It's been amazing and it sparked a new found passion for the job. I got a chance to speak with Chuck's son and asked him to please accept me for who I am and to understand that I'm not his competition. He may need some time to get there, but I think the world of him, so let's pray God softens his heart.

One of the things that really surprised me was how long it took to get acclimated back into "normal" life. My senses are so much more acute. I notice things I never noticed before. I was outside one day and a helicopter flew above me and I froze. No reason to freeze but I did. Whenever I pass a police patrol car, I get a sick feeling in my stomach and I have the strongest urge to stop that car. Deep inside me there is the need to tell them I'm no longer that disrespectful punk kid I was before. I want them to know that I'm a different person. I am not that other Michael anymore.

The other thing that surprised me was I hadn't really thought about the "time" I had in prison. My Aunt Bonnie was so right when she said, "You now have the time to devote to yourself, what else do you have to do"? I didn't appreciate the "time" I had. I thought it was a negative in my life. Instead, it became a definite positive that, ironically, I miss. Well, I mean I miss the opportunity of actually having time to devote to myself. With working long days and an 8 p.m. curfew, the days fly by. At the end of my day, there really isn't any "time" left. That has been one of the most difficult things I've had to come to terms with. The challenge has been to find how to incorporate all the things that I need to complete my life in the hours I have. First, I have to identify those things. My dreams include finding a welcoming Church-home like my prison church. I absolutely know I have to find a way to reach those who are faced with addictions. Those people who feel that there is no way to escape their demons. Drug use takes you to very dark places. It changes you from the inside out. You actually start believing that you are unable to overcome the depths. I want people to understand that kind of thinking is actually the devil working his black magic. You see, the devil is in a life and death struggle for every soul he can steal from God so he works unrelentingly.

One of the biggest hurdles has been to overcome the reputation I left behind. I was really surprised by the fact that people expected me to pick up where I left off. It never occurred to them that I would change over time and that I would not be the same person who left years ago. It has been difficult to convince them that I am no longer the old Michael. I no longer want the drug scene and the fast life. Women are fearful of me. How many times had I discussed this very topic in the seminars I gave? How many times did we talk about how hard it would be to win back trust? I said the words, but I guess I was guilty of thinking it was true for the other inmates but somehow I was exempt. I am not exempt, it does include me. Trust building takes time and patience. You already know that patience is not my one of my strengths. But, only through time can I prove that I am trustworthy. I have to remind myself of that every day.

Shortly after I got home, I went to the YMCA. I wanted to continue the workout program I started in prison. The female clerk asked for my ID. I handed it to her and she looked up at me and asked, "What is this?" I had to explain it was a government-issued non-driver's ID. To make a long story short, I left the YMCA that day without working out. The trust issue touches us in every corner of our lives. It will just take time.

I recently ran into a very successful business man I knew before I went away. He said to me, "Michael, how long were you gone"? I responded, "Five years and eight months, Sir." That's when he said, "God, you just lost five years and eight months of your life." I looked straight into his eyes and with words that came directly from my heart

I said, "No, Sir, those years could have been lost if I had chosen to let that happen but instead I accepted the fact that I had some major work to do on myself and I put those years to very good use." Then we shook hands and he told me to be sure to call him in the spring so we could discuss future business. I left our meeting smiling from ear to ear. Yes, it will just take time.

I have learned I will never again sell life short. It's amazing to finally have the maturity and ability to determine what is important and what's not. What's real and what's imaginary. What is reachable and what isn't worth the effort. It's good to have dreams and to know they are attainable. Giving back to my community is an absolute must for me. It's not clear to me yet how I will accomplish that. I am hopeful that it will be through the church or possibly through working or volunteering in a drug court or a half-way house. In October 2012, I attended a Sunday service at St. Monica's. Father Ray spotted me before Mass began. He came right over and looked me sternly in the eye and said, "Michael, where have you been? We need you to get serious here because I want you to start preaching on the weekends." I looked at him and said, "Me, Father"? He replied, "Yes, you are the one with the story and God will guide you on the path to help touch all these people who need to hear your message." Just like that, I received the answer to my prayers. I had been praying for a way to be able to reach out to young people and to help the next "Michael" learn before he ends up in prison or, worse, dies much too early. I know first-hand how harmful drugs are and the dangerous situations in which you place yourself when you use drugs. Every addiction is harmful but I am proof that addiction can be overcome and I know God is great all the time and there isn't anything that He can't take care of.

I have been so blessed that I have another chance to live on the outside of the prison walls. I will never take freedom for granted ever again. I will never forget my past, but I will always remember that just because today might not be the best of days, it beats all of the past days. I hope this book proves that a comeback and recovery is absolutely possible and that a clean and sober life is the only way to go. You don't have to prove anything to God. He loves you just the way you are—even if you are addicted to drugs and alcohol

Thank you for reading my story and I hope God's light shines on you always.

"Because one believes in oneself, one doesn't try to convince others. Because one is content with oneself, one doesn't need others' approval. Because one accepts oneself, the whole world accepts him." —*Lao Tzu*

Afterword

HERE IS A SAMPLE THE group presentations I gave in 2011 as well as a sermon. I was so proud to deliver these at Mid-State Correctional Facility during my incarceration. I have also included a 2012 sermon I was asked to give at St Monica's Church in Rochester, NY shortly after I was released. Last, but not least, I have included my "famous" Tando-licious" microwave cheesecake recipe.

I am not only proud of this work but totally amazed by it, especially when I think back to the years that drug addiction overpowered me and held me hostage to a life of total darkness. It is only now that I can truly understand just how far I came. Finding my way back to God has been one of the greatest accomplishments of my life.

So you think you know football, prove it!

March 2011

The room was filled with 45 inmates, three counselors and one correctional officer. My "assistant," Cheech announced to the inmates, "Please arrange your seats in two rows facing each other just like it would be if you were in a football stadium." The inmates set up the rows of chairs on opposites sides of a 50 x 30 foot room. The reasoning for this was to give them a feeling of excitement and change. They never sit like this. My theory was that the smallest change a person makes is the one that counts. Once the room was set up, Cheech turned a large chalk board around so the group could see the display that my partner, Mr. Craig Henry and I set up the night before. On the board was the name of the seminar, a poster of my role model, Thomas Henderson, along with some of his words of inspiration, hope and recovery. You could feel the anticipation building. Lastly, Cheech turned on the community boom box with a cassette of instrumental music and our recovery "rap" song.

Before we walked on "stage," Mr. Henry and I prayed together. Craig prayed to Allah and I prayed to Jesus. We were dressed in our prison best. We wore freshly pressed white shirts and our best ties. We dressed the part because in recovery you are supposed to enjoy life. These outfits spoke volumes. I was able to borrow a rubber football from the recreation department. So with the football prop in my hand, we began.

The audience was a very unique group of individuals. At least 90% were on some type of medication for their mental health issues. Ordinarily, most of the guys are back asleep by 9 a.m. because they would have taken their morning meds. Not this morning. You would have thought that each had drunk a pot of coffee. Each inmate was attentive and eager to hear what we had to say. As we entered the room, the guys stood as we walked between the two rows of inmates each chanting the *Recovery Rap.* The excitement mounted as the audience joined in the song.

I just woke up and having a bad day,
Thankful to be alive, able to see another day,
Only thing I'm not thankful for is this monkey on my back.
It took all my money and left me feigning for some crack…

I walked to the center of the room and got down into a football stance just like a center for a professional football team while Mr. Henry called out the first three steps from an Alcoholics Anonymous Meeting. Then he threw me a touchdown pass. The room went crazy! Everyone was pumped up, fired up and motivated. Now it was time for business.

"So You Think You Know Football, Prove It," was a seminar designed to teach the inmates how important it is to build a strong team of people around you, each of whom is also striving to reach recovery. Just like a football team, you can't win all by yourself. We need people we can rely on when things don't go our way. The beautiful part about recovery is there is always someone with arms wide open to help us with our journey. We just have to reach out for them.

I used the football as the main prop. Whenever someone would ask a question, or we asked for feedback, we would throw them the ball. Once the inmate received the ball it was his turn to talk. They loved the idea of having the football passed to them because inmates don't get a chance to do things like this every day. This was different, just like change; it was something new for the day. During the entire seminar, I could see that everyone was really into it. They gave full attention and that is huge for these guys. Then, I passed the ball to a guy who had been struggling to stay clean and sober for the past 20 years. Once he had the ball he just sat there and we could see that he was searching the depths of his heart. As soon as he started to speak, tears started to well up in his eyes. It was my first time seeing a man cry during one of my seminars. I was startled a little bit. Fortunately, before the seminar my counselor, Mr. Kogel, said to me, "Mr. Tandoi, if anyone should start to cry, let them. Don't stop the flow of that river that they have built up inside of them." So, when I did see the tears I just waited patiently and when the time was right, I offered compassion. When this man was done crying he got up, I passed him the ball again, and he scored a touchdown with a huge sigh of relief. And, the "fans" cheered! It was the touchdown of his lifetime.

For me, my new life is all about giving back. The Lord has given me a voice and the courage to use it. The feeling I get every time I do a seminar is amazing. When I speak, I give from my heart so I never have to worry about being phony. This gift is so genuine that at times I can actually feel my body being lifted off the ground. God, Recovery, Inspiration, and Motivation are the miracle mix I fell in love with during my own incarceration.

Genesis 4:6

July 2011

> *The Lord asked Cain, "Why are you so angry? Why do you look so dejected? You will be accepted if you do what is right. But if you refuse to do what is right, then watch out! Sin is couching at your door, eager to control you. But you must subdue it and be its master."*

Today I want to talk about letting go of anger and bitterness; that inner hatred that creates darkness within us where the devil can find a home. We allow the devil a way in and he consumes us little by little. We tend to believe this feeling is normal and okay. Sometimes we walk around life without realizing that this anger exists within us. That darkness weighs us down to a point where it becomes unbearable.

Cain was jealous because his brother Abel's offering was accepted and his was not. God didn't abash Cain's character, he simply said, "Be patient, Cain, and the next time you offer me a sacrifice make it right."

Sin is crouching at your door. WATCH OUT! Don't we understand sin is everywhere? If we don't protect ourselves every day, we will get attacked.

Ephesians 6:10: *Be strong in the Lord and in his mighty power. Put on all of God's armor so that you will be able to stand firm against all strategies of the devil.*

I love this prayer and I say it every morning. *Saint Michael the Archangel, defend us in battle. Be our defense against the wickedness and the snares of the devil. May God rebuke him we humbly pray, and do thou, O Prince of the Heavenly Host, by the power of God, cast out Satan and the other evil spirits who prowl about the world for the ruination of souls. Amen.*

Wow! Romans 6:12: *Do not let sin control the way you live, do not give into sinful desires. Do not let any part of your body become an instrument of evil to serve sin. Instead, give yourselves completely to God, for you were dead, but now you have new life.* So use your whole body as an instrument to do what is right for the glory of God. Sin is no longer your master, for you no longer live under the requirements of the law. Instead, you live under the freedom of God's grace.

Let me fill you in on the little secret that God has revealed to me and many others. God doesn't want us to live in anger and hatred, bitterness and jealously. He doesn't want us to be ugly within. He created us to be pure and sincere and to love with compassion through his Son, Jesus. He gave us Jesus, His only Son, so that our sins could be washed away. When you are faced with a situation that can cause you to become sinful, turn to the Lord and give it all to him. That is the secret.

Jesus said in Matthew 11:28: *Come to me all you who are weary and burdened, give it to me, and I, the Lord, will give you rest.* Everything, whatever the situation may be, as hard as it may get, let go! I'm telling you it is worth it and the feeling is so refreshing. Don't allow the devil to hold you down. He will try to form your body into concrete. A hold like that was never meant to be formed around your body. Like quicksand the devil wants to take us all down, all the way down to his fiery pit.

We can do things God's way and receive his blessings, or we can do things our way and suffer the consequences.

James 4:7-8: *Humble yourselves before God and resist the devil and he will flee from you. Come close to God and God will come close to you, wash your hands, you sinners purify your hearts for your loyalty is divided between God and the world.*

When we hold onto our anger, do you honestly think it affects anyone other than ourselves? No! The only person we hurt is ourselves and we cheat ourselves out of the true blessing that God has planned for us.

Psalm 46: *God is our refuge and strength, always ready to help us in times of trouble.* When we let go of that sin that is crouching at our door, we actually open the door to everlasting life. The reward of letting go becomes limitless--beyond our wildest dreams. Don't hide behind the door because you are afraid. Take a chance and turn whatever may be holding you down over to God.

John 7:4: *You can't become famous if you hide like this. If you can do such wonderful things, show yourself.*

Just how great is our God? So great, that we have eternal life through Jesus Christ. Anger and bitterness, hatred, jealousy, and evil intentions towards others are completely directed by the devil. He is solely responsible for that ugliness that lives within us. His main goal is to steal away our happiness. The devil is eager to control you and me. More than anything else he wants to destroy our life and ultimately take our last breath.

Matthew 7:13: *You can enter God's kingdom only through the narrow gate. The highway to Satan is broad and its gate is wide for many who choose that way, but the gateway to life is very narrow and the road is difficult and only a few enter it.*

You choose. Will it be life or death? Will it be prosperity and success or disaster and destruction?

Genesis 4:6: ends with: *You must subdue it and be its master.* Jesus Christ is the only answer. He will cast out all our demons by giving us the ability to overcome all our life situations. He is stronger and more powerful than Satan. Today, allow God to tie him up and let's plunder his house. We can destroy Satan by praising God. Whenever the devil tries to attack, don't let him in. Remember the Armor of God will protect you from evil.

I would like to finish by telling you the story called "The Brick." A young and successful executive was traveling down a neighborhood street, going a bit too fast in his new Jaguar. He was watching for kids darting out from between parked cards and slowed down when he thought he saw something. As his car passed, no children appeared. Instead a brick smashed into the Jag's side door. He slammed on the brakes and backed the Jag to the spot where the brick had been thrown.

The angry driver then jumped out of the car, grabbed the nearest kid and pushed him up against a parked car shouting, "What was that all about and who are you? This is a new car and that brick you threw is going to cost a lot of money to fix the damage. Why did you do it"? The young boy was apologetic. "Please, mister, please. I'm sorry but I didn't know what else to do, he pleaded. I threw the brick because no one else would stop." With tears dripping down his face and off his chin, the youth pointed to the spot just around a parked car. "It's my brother, he rolled off the curb and fell out of his wheelchair and I can't lift him up."

Now sobbing the boy asked the stunned executive, "Would you please help me get him back into his wheelchair? He's hurt and too heavy for me."

Moved beyond words, the driver tried to swallow the rapidly swelling lump in his throat. He hurriedly lifted the handicapped boy back into his wheelchair, then took out a linen handkerchief and dabbed at the boy's fresh scrapes and cuts. A quick look told him everything was going to be okay. "Thank you and God bless you," the grateful child told the stranger. Too shook up for words, the man simply watched the boy push his wheelchair-bound brother down the sidewalk towards their home.

It was a long, slow walk back to the Jaguar. The damage was very noticeable, but the driver never bothered to repair the dented door. He kept the dent there to remind him of this message. Don't go through life so fast that someone has to throw a brick at you to get your attention. God whispers in our souls and speaks to our hearts. Sometimes when we don't have time to listen, he throws a brick at us. It's our choice to listen or not.

Thought of the day: If God had a refrigerator your picture would be on it. If he had a wallet, your photo would be in it. He sends you flowers every spring. He sends you a sunrise every morning. Face it, friend,—He is crazy about you.

Let us pray. Father God, Lord Jesus, thank you so much for creating a magical feeling inside of our hearts. Thank you for your son, Jesus Christ who shines through all of us every day. Whenever sin sneaks up on us please, Lord, fill us with your love and protect us from evil. We ask this in the name of Jesus who lives and reigns with us and the Holy Spirit. Amen.

Captivity

November 2012

Father God, Lord Jesus , Mother Mary, all my angels and saints please give me the ability and strength to deliver the message of true transformation, as I was one who once was lost, living for all the wrong reasons, following the path of destruction and disaster, the life that we call darkness. You gave me a second chance, Lord, to live and as I stand here today at Saint Monica's Church please allow your light, the light of Christ, to shine not only on me but everyone present here today. Lord, today grant us courage to stand up and break out of any restraints that may be holding us back from a deeper relationship with you. Amen

Imagine this …..you hear a voice shouting in the wilderness telling you to prepare the way for the Lord Jesus Christ. That same voice screams out that valleys will be filled, mountains and hills will be made level, curves will be straightened and rough places made smooth. If we witnessed this in today's world we would think this man, John the Baptist, was out of his mind crazy. He was screaming out this message just so we would know that a man named Jesus Christ was coming to us as our ultimate Savior. Jesus would show us the way to salvation, victory over evil, and achievement of success and prosperity,

Before we go on, let me tell you a little bit about myself. I was sent to prison for 7 years and by the grace of God I served 5 years and 8 months for a high speed car chase while I was under the influence of crack cocaine. Yes, I was addicted to drugs and alcohol. It took me a number of years in prison to finally hit rock bottom. When I had nowhere else to go and I couldn't find another wall to hit, I knew it was time for a change. However, I still had no idea what that meant. I knew nothing about recovery or of change and very little about God. I knew nothing about who I really was or even how I felt. I couldn't even identify how I wanted to feel. I'd been under a spell for so many years that I just got accustomed to living on the dark side of life.

I can remember one night in particular, during my incarceration, when I was placed in solitary confinement due to my behavior. Solitary confinement is a 10 x 6 cell, known as the "box." I found myself down on my knees praying to God to help me with the charges for which I was being accused. I never in a million years could have predicted all that would happen to me. Unfortunately, I was one of those people who had to learn things the hard way. Actually, I was one of those people who had to learn in the hardest of ways. But, learn I did. Looking back now I understand how deeply I had strayed and how disrespectful of myself and everyone else I had been. I finally began to feel the pain from my mistakes and the bad choices I had made. I actually ached inside because I now could recognize how much God truly had blessed me from the very beginning of my life, yet, I had never stopped long enough to recognize the gift. I took full advantage of everyone and everything. I selected every wrong road in my fanatical quest for acceptance. But before that night, when I prayed to God to save me, those concepts had never occurred to me. The only way I can explain my former life is to say that those were the blind years. Love was unknown to me because I never took the time to learn how to love and respect myself first. Michael got lost because he was too busy reaching for the next shiny object.

God says in Deuteronomy 30:15 : *Today I am giving you the choice between life and death, between prosperity and disaster. For I command you this day to love the Lord your God and to keep his commands, decrees, and regulations by walking in his ways. If you do this you will live and multiply, and the Lord your God will bless you* … choose life.

I would like everyone to realize that you don't have to go to prison to become a captive. No matter where we are in our lives we can become captives, held in bondage, held from growth with our Lord, Jesus Christ. It could be a bad relationship, an unhappy marriage, a small hidden lie, a dirty habit. The list goes on and on. Only you as an individual know what's keeping you from that everlasting freedom Christ offers. My last three years in prison were the best years of my life because my heart was free, my vision was free, my voice, like John the Baptist, was being heard because that's what the Lord had planned. In a place that breeds darkness I was able to find light.

In Mark11:22 Jesus said to his disciples, *Have faith in God. I tell you the truth, you can say to this mountain, may you be lifted up and thrown into*

154

the sea, and it will be happen. If you have faith as small as a mustard seed you can say to this mountain move from here to there, or to that hill be leveled or to that curve straighten. This is what John the Baptist was preaching before the coming of Christ. He already knew because God sent him a revelation. But here's the secret ingredient; you must believe it will happen and have no doubt in your heart. I tell you, you can pray for anything and if you believe that you'll receive it, it will be yours.

Jesus Christ makes everything possible for all of us. Today, ask God to remove the mountain, the hill, or the jagged edge and straighten out your path. Don't be afraid to get down on your knees and cry out to the Lord. Ask and you shall receive, seek and you shall find, knock and the doors will be open. If you're still living in darkness, today's your day to break free. Don't be lost anymore. Jesus says, "Come to me all of you who are weary and burdened and I shall give you rest." Amen.

Last but not least, here is the recipe I created for Microwave Cheesecake. It is one of the recipes that inspired the phase, "Tandoi dishes are Tando-licious." Enjoy!

Fifteen Minutes in Heaven Microwave Cheesecake

5 packages 3 oz cream cheese

15 Duplex cookies (like Oreos)

16 Oatmeal cookies

½ can (10.5 oz) of condensed milk

3 oz of Nutri banana drink

1 c granulated sugar

Margarine spread

Strawberry jam

1. Scrape and discard the cream from the cookies

2. In 2 quart microwave bowl heat duplex and oatmeal cookies till soften (about 45 seconds), then crush cookies to a fine crush.

3. Start with ½ c of margarine and add to cookie until cookies are moist and form a crust. Add more margarine as needed.

4. Place cream cheese in a separate bowl and microwave just until cheese is soften about 20 seconds.

5. Mix condensed milk with Nutri banana drink until blended. Add granulated sugar and mix until smooth.

6. In a 2 quart glass container, form cookie crust 2 inches high around container. Then pour cream cheese mixture from center of container.

7. Microwave 15 minutes on power level 2 or 3. If cake is rising or cooking too fast, reduce power level.

8. Remove from microwave and spread cake with strawberry jam and place in refrigerator to cool.

PEACE TO ALL OF YOU.

Author Biography

BONNIE TRAVAGLINI, Michael Tandoi's aunt, chronicles Michael's journey from childhood through his lengthy drug addiction and his eventual incarceration as he fights to reestablish his relationship with God and search for the man he was destined to be. This is a story of recovery and hope. Michael and Bonnie reside in New York State.

Printed in the United States
by Baker & Taylor Publisher Services